Professional Accounting Technician Apprenticeship

Synoptic Workbook

Sheriden Amos

Published by Osborne Books Limited
Tel 01905 748071
Email books@osbornebooks.co.uk
Website www.osbornebooks.co.uk

Design by Laura Ingham

Printed by CPI Group (UK) Limited, Croydon, CR0 4YY, on environmentally friendly, acid-free paper from managed forests.

FSC www.fsc.org MIX Paper | Supporting responsible forestry FSC® C013604

British Library Cataloguing in Publication Data
A catalogue record for this book is available from the British Library

ISBN 978-1-911681-09-0

Contents

Introduction

AAT PROFESSIONAL ACCOUNTING TECHNICIAN APPRENTICESHIP

The AAT Professional Accounting Technician Apprenticeship covers high-level accounting and finance topics and tasks. It includes a wide range of financial management skills and applications; drafting financial statements for limited companies; recommending accounting systems strategy; and constructing and presenting complex management accounting reports.

The AAT Professional Accounting Technician Apprenticeship standard requires two elements to be completed: on programme learning and end point assessment.

On programme learning - the AAT Diploma in Professional Accounting

The apprenticeship requires on programme learning and the AAT Diploma in Professional Accounting qualification ensures the students will gain the required knowledge, skills, and behaviours within the apprenticeship.

End point assessment (EPA)

At the end of the apprenticeship, students must complete:

- A synoptic assessment, covering the knowledge and skills in the apprenticeship specification.
- A portfolio and reflective discussion or written statement.

This book provides practice for the synoptic assessment.

SYNOPTIC ASSESSMENT COVERAGE

The synoptic assessment covers the knowledge and skills in the AAT Diploma in Professional Accounting qualification.

The synoptic assessment for the AAT Professional Accounting Technician Apprenticeship has five assessment objectives that are detailed below:

AO1 Demonstrate an understanding of the roles and responsibilities of the accounting function within an organisation and examine ways of preventing and detecting fraud and systemic weaknesses.

AO2 Evaluate an organisation's accounting control systems and procedures.

AO3 Analyse an organisation's decision making and control using management accounting tools.

AO4 Analyse an organisation's decision-making and control using ratio analysis.

AO5 Analyse the internal controls of an organisation and make recommendations.

SYNOPTIC ASSESSMENT STRUCTURE

The synoptic assessment for the AAT Professional Accounting Technician Apprenticeship is a computer-based assessment that is partially computer-marked and partially human-marked. The live synoptic assessment is three hours long.

Students are provided with pre-release material that is made available to them ahead of their assessment. This material is designed to contextualise the tasks in the synoptic assessment. Studying this material will encourage students to think about the assessment topics in an integrated way, which is necessary for performing well in the synoptic assessment.

Students will not be able to take a copy of the pre-release material into the assessment. However, access to this material will be available through pop-up windows in the assessment. All live assessments will be based on a single piece of pre-release material.

WHAT THIS BOOKS CONTAINS

This book provides four full Practice Synoptic Assessments to prepare the student for the live Computer Based Assessment. They are based directly on the structure, style and content of the sample assessment material provided by AAT at www.aat.org.uk.

Each of the four practice assessments is based on a different company and the pre-release material included will be unique to each practice assessment. This will provide students a good idea of the types of scenarios that could form the basis of the live assessment.

Students should read the pre-release material before they attempt each practice assessment in this book in the same way as they will when they sit their live assessment.

The AAT practice assessment material provides a breakdown of the marks allocated to each task. This helps students to appreciate the relative importance of each task in the assessment and to plan how long to spend on each one. The Practice Synoptic Assessments in this book also show the mark allocation for each task.

Suggested answers to the Practice Assessments are set out in this book.

ACKNOWLEDGEMENT

The author would like to thank Celia Laverick for providing some of the material included in this book.

Practice synoptic assessment 1

Pre-release material

Company background and history

Adams and Blackwall Ltd (ABL) is a heating servicing and maintenance company, operating throughout the West Country.

The company is run from a head office on an industrial estate in Exeter and from seven branches throughout the region.

ABL was established in the early 1990s by two of its current directors, James Adams and Hazel Adams (Née Blackwall). James and Hazel are majority shareholders. Shares are also held by the other directors and key employees who are encouraged to acquire them through an employee share scheme.

Starting with a single branch in Exeter, the company has grown organically, gradually establishing its branch network throughout the region.

In 20-5 the company had revenue of £22 million and employed 370 FTE employees, 280 of whom were qualified engineers, the rest trainees, site support and office staff. In 20-5 ABL won a contract which involved significant work in the Barnstaple area. This has initially been covered by other branches, but the opening of a branch in Barnstaple was agreed for January 20-6, both to expand the business and to ensure the profitability of the contract.

Mission statement

To be the best heating servicing and maintenance company in the region.

We aim to provide the highest possible level of service to clients, completing installations on time and attending call-outs as speedily as possible, always treating clients with courtesy and respect.

We operate to high ethical standards and aim to promote sustainability both with clients and through the way we do business.

Developments in the market

The dismantling of council housing and council in-house maintenance which started in the 1980s is ongoing. Cuts in council budgets and growth in housing associations providing social housing have led to growth in the industry. However, competition is keen and margins on tenders can be very tight.

Renewable energy systems have been very much in demand. ABL has invested in MCS accreditation (an industry standard "Microgeneration Certification Scheme"), and also in staff training, in order to be able to compete in this new sector of the market and has seen promising growth in this area. However, recent government cuts in subsidies for renewables make this sector of the market less certain.

Strategic planning

Long-term success is felt to be dependent on both successful retendering to existing clients as well as winning new long-term clients. The company uses the 'balanced scorecard' to assess its overall performance:

Learning and growth

Staff retention is good.

Staff development and progression – ABL runs an apprenticeship scheme which commonly leads to qualification and employment as an engineer. In 20-5 eight engineers were promoted to senior engineers, and the Exeter Senior Engineer was promoted to Operations Director taking over this role from James Adams who had previously combined this role with that of Managing Director. All engineers are on the Gas Safe Register and 25% have now completed MCS training (up from 20% in 20-4).

Business processes

The efficiency of a servicing engineer is measured in terms of average call outs per week. This declines when engineers are covering a wide area and so need to spend significant amounts of time travelling. The establishment of the new branch at Barnstaple should improve efficiency.

In 20-5, speed limiters were introduced to company vans for all branches other than Exeter (where travel is mainly around the city). This has helped to cut fuel costs.

Customers

During 20-5 ABL lost 2% of its long-term clients in retendering. It gained several new clients during the year and its overall client base has grown by 3% over 20-5. Several housing associations have been through periods of growth and ABL has benefited from this growth.

Financial

Revenue grew by 11% in 20-5. The gross profit margin remained fairly stable despite downward pressure on bid prices tendered. Dividends paid to shareholders grew in proportion to sales growth. ABL is funded largely by retained earnings.

Strategic mapping

Management believe that continued focus both on staff development and staff progression in the firm will ensure the continued success of the business. Expansion of the branch network to increase business efficiency gives additional opportunities for staff to be promoted to more senior roles within the firm. In addition, the expansion should enable better customer service and improve customer retention. Expansion of staff capabilities with regard to the installation and maintenance of renewable energy systems will also be a basis for future growth.

Staff

ABL's key staff are as follows:

Managing Director (MD)	James Adams
Operations Director (OD)	Philip Evans
Sales Director (SD)	Ruby Wentworth
Finance Director (FD)	Richard Johns
Human Resources Director (HRD)	Hazel Adams

All branch managers report to the Operations Director, as do the senior engineers.

The FD heads up the Accounts Department which includes a Management Accountant who is responsible for budgeting and costing activities, and a Financial Accountant who is responsible for producing statutory accounts and returns and overseeing the work of the accounts clerks. There are four accounts clerks – a Payroll Clerk, Accounts Payable Clerk, Accounts Receivable Clerk and an Accounts Assistant.

ABL's financial statements

ABL Statement of profit or loss for the year ended 31.12.20-5

Continuing operations	£000
Revenue	22,500
Cost of sales	19,100
Gross profit	3,400
Operating expenses	2,320
Operating profit	1,080
Finance costs	40
Profit before tax	1,040
Tax	240
Profit for the period from continuing operations	800

ABL Statement of financial position as at 31.12.20-5

	£000
Assets	
Non-Current assets	
Plant, property and equipment	625
Current assets	
Inventories	1,075
Trade receivables	4,610
Cash and cash equivalents	690
	7,000
Equities and liabilities	
Ordinary share capital (£1 shares)	480
Retained earnings	3,620
Non-current liabilities	
Loans	500
Current liabilities	
Trade payables	2,200
Taxation	200
	7,000

INSTRUCTIONS

The Practice Assessment contains five tasks and you should attempt to complete every task.

Read every task carefully to make sure you understand what is required.

Where the date is relevant, it is given in the task data.

Both minus signs and brackets can be used to indicate negative numbers unless task instructions state otherwise.

You must use a full stop to indicate a decimal point. For example, write 100.57, not 100,57 or 100 57.

You may use a comma to indicate a number in the thousands, but you don't have to. For example, 10000 and 10,000 are both acceptable.

You have three hours to complete the Practice Assessment.

TASKS

Task 1: 20 marks

(a) Management accounts are produced for several reasons. Identify which of these are valid purposes for management accounts, and which are not.

Purpose		**Valid**	**Not valid**
(a)	To monitor current costs against budget		
(b)	To comply with International Accounting Standards		
(c)	To monitor liquidity		
(d)	To detect fraud		
(e)	To comply with statutory obligations to report results		

(5 marks)

(b) The Accounts Assistant uses completed job cards to prepare sales invoices for maintenance work. These list details of the engineer who carried out the work, the work done and the parts that were used. The Accounts Assistant discovers that one job card has not been signed by the customer on completion of the work.

What is the correct action for the Accounts Assistant to take?

(a)	Prepare the sales invoice as normal	
(b)	Prepare the sales invoice as normal, but also keep a copy of the job card and send the original back to the relevant Branch Manager for investigation	
(c)	Prepare the sales invoice as normal, but also keep a copy of the job card and send the original back to the relevant Engineer for investigation	

(2 marks)

(c) The Accounts Payable Clerk asks you to state whether the following errors and omissions would be detected by reconciling suppliers' statements to the supplier accounts payable ledger account.

Error/Omission		**Would be detected**	**Would not be detected**
(a)	A purchase invoice is omitted from a supplier's account		
(b)	A purchase invoice is posted to the wrong supplier's account		
(c)	A supplier sends in an invoice for goods/services which were not received		
(d)	The supplier's invoice charges higher amounts than agreed		
(e)	An inputting error has been made when recording the amount of a purchase invoice		
(f)	A cheque payment made to the supplier has been debited to a customer's account		

(6 marks)

(d) The Accounts Payable Clerk receives an email from a large supplier. The email says that the supplier has changed its bank account details and requests that future payments be made to a new bank account.

What actions should the Accounts Payable Clerk take?

(a)	Check that the email is from a valid email address for the supplier in question	
(b)	Ask for a letter on supplier headed paper signed by a known signatory confirming the request	
(c)	Call the supplier by phone to confirm the details	
(d)	Get authorisation for the change from the Financial Accountant	
(e)	All of the above	

(2 marks)

(e) You have been asked to review some proposed policies to determine if they promote ethical and sustainable practices at ABL.

Policy	**Would promote**	**Would not promote**
Implement a price increase of 5% for all existing private customers when costs have increased by 2%		✓
Ask all qualified engineers to identify additional training requirements they have	✓	

(2 marks)

(f) Complete the following statement about stakeholders and the use of financial information by choosing the correct option:

Internal / External information does not need to comply with accounting standards. If the business is planning to open more branches, the **directors / bank** will make this type of decision. To monitor this decision, it will use **the statement of profit or loss / budgeted reports by branch**.

(3 marks)

Task 2: 20 marks

You have been asked to review the adequacy of ABL's controls over capital expenditure and payroll.

(a) Identify whether each of the following control activities would help ensure that non-current assets are safeguarded and accurately recorded.

Activity		**Would help**	**Would not help**
(a)	Disposals of capital items must be authorised by a director		
(b)	A capital budget is approved by the directors as part of the annual budget process		
(c)	The non-current asset register is reconciled to the general ledger each month		
(d)	Three quotes are required for purchases of non-current assets above £10,000		
(e)	Depreciation is calculated by the Financial Controller, who is AAT qualified		

(5 marks)

Your review of payroll has established the following procedures.

Procedures over staff recruitment and staff costs in the branch

- Branches use a job costing software package called Userve to record and manage jobs that engineers attend. Recording starts with a quote and progresses as actual costs are reported. The overall profitability of individual jobs is monitored both at the branch and by Head Office.
- At each branch, engineers submit weekly timesheets to Branch Managers who check information to Userve before signing timesheets to approve them and passing them to a branch clerk for authorising on Userve.
- Timesheets are filed at the branch. Hours recorded are picked up from Userve and input into the payroll software at head office by the Payroll Clerk.
- Branch office staff are required to complete weekly timesheets which are signed by branch managers before being scanned and emailed to head office where details are input into the payroll software by the Payroll Clerk.
- Recruitment of new staff is normally managed by Human Resources (HR) at head office, but occasionally a branch manager will employ an additional member of staff on a temporary basis without authorisation from head office. This is mainly for cleaners or engineers who are required to cover staff sickness on an emergency basis. No follow up checks are made by head office.

Payroll software and processing

- The company uses "Sage Payroll" to perform all payroll processing. The Payroll Clerk is fully trained in this system and the Financial Accountant has completed basic training in it. Access to the system is password protected, the Payroll Clerk has full user rights and the Financial Accountant has administrator rights.

- The Payroll Clerk is responsible for inputting all timesheets received before the 25th of each month onto the payroll system and for running the monthly payroll. Employees are paid by BACS on the last working day of the month.
- Payroll printouts, along with the BACS payment authority, are produced by the Payroll Clerk and passed to the Financial Accountant for approval. The Financial Accountant checks that the payroll prints agree to the BACS schedule and that the total amount is in line with the previous month; significant discrepancies are investigated.
- Back-up copies of payroll data are stored on site in a fireproof safe.

(b) **(i)** Identify FIVE systemic weaknesses in ABL's internal controls for payroll. (5 marks)

(ii) Explain how each weakness that you have identified could create a problem for the company. (10 marks)

Note: You are **not** required to make recommendations to change the procedures.

Weaknesses	**Potential problem for the company**
1 only significant discrepancies are investigated	Some small wrong entries could begin to mount up as they are unchecked.
2 Employing temporary unauthorised members of Staff.	unauthorised members of Staff could not have had the correct training (liability)
3 No follow up checks done by head office.	irresponsible and could end up with problems for the company
4 only one person has full access to the payroll system	They could be making unauthorised changes and no one would know.
5 Back up copies stored in a fire proof safe.	would be safer if these were kept computerised.

Task 3: 20 marks 20

The Managing Director, James Adams, wants to improve the sales of solar panel scheme move to grow the microgeneration part of the business. He has heard value analysis and val could improve process and profitability, as part of target costing.

(a) Identify whether each of the following statements in relation to value analysis, value engineering and target costing is true or false.

Statement	**True/False**
Value engineering is used to design new products and services at the lowest possible cost	T
Using value analysis on existing products will always result in the quality being kept the same or improved	F
Value engineering is for both existing and new products	T
Value analysis considers how value is provided to the customer	T
Value engineering and value analysis focus on the elements of a product that do not contribute to the value of the product	F

(5 marks) 1

ABL is considering developing a new, more energy-efficient heating system, based on purchased photovoltaic (pv) panels and a new type of heating system controller. The following information is available.

System development and testing, including working with a system controller designer and manufacturer, would cost £200,000 immediately, and a further £150,000 in one year's time.

Marketing would initially cost £100,000 and then a further £50,000 a year for the next four years.

On average, variable costs per system would be £5,800 and each system would sell for an average of £7,000.

Fixed costs relating solely to this system would be £80,000 for each year it was sold. Purchase of pv panels and controllers and sales of completed systems will take place in the same year.

Fixed costs of £1,500,000 related to other services have already been incurred and will continue.

Estimated sales of the system are (Year 0 being the start of the project):

Year 1	800
Year 2	600
Year 3	300
Year 4	100

There will be no sales after year 4.

(b) Complete the table below, which includes the discount factors for the company's cost of capital of 8%, to determine whether the new system is worthwhile. Carry out calculations in £ thousands. Enter cash outflows as negative figures and cash inflows as positive.

Year	**0**	**1**	**2**	**3**	**4**
	£000	£000	£000	£000	£000
System development					
Marketing					
Sales revenue					
Variable costs					
Fixed costs					
Net total for year					
Discount factor 8%					
Present value					
Net present value					

(8 marks)

(c) Explain whether ABL should develop the new systems or not.

(2 marks)

(d) Discuss the commercial factors that could impact on ABL that underpin the life cycle of the new system.

(5 marks)

Task 4: 20 marks 20

(a) Use the extract from the financial statements shown below to complete the calculations of financial ratios in the table on the next page.

(10 marks)

ABL Statement of profit or loss		
	Year ended 31.12.20-4	**Year ended 31.12.20-5**
	£000	£000
Revenue	20,250	22,500
Gross profit	3,139	3,400
Operating profit	931	1,080
ABL Statement of financial position		
Assets		
Non-current assets	650	625
Inventories	970	1,075
Trade receivables	4,327	4,610
Cash and cash equivalents	553	690
	6,500	7,000
Equities and liabilities		
Equity	3,718	4,100
Non-current liabilities	500	500
Trade payables	2,110	2,200
Taxation	172	200
	6,500	7,000

Ratios

Show profitability, financial position, and liquidity ratios to one decimal place. Working capital ratios should be rounded to the nearest day.

Complete the shaded boxes.

Ratio	**Year ended 31.12.20-4**	**Year ended 31.12.20-5**
Profitability (correct to 1 decimal place)		
Gross profit margin %	15.5%	15.1%
Operating profit margin %	4.6%	4.8%
Return on capital employed	22.1%	
Financial position (correct to 1 decimal place)		
Gearing	11.9%	
Liquidity (correct to 1 decimal place)		
Quick/acid test ratio	2.1:1	
Working capital management (correct to the nearest day)		
Inventory holding period	21 days	
Trade receivables collection period	78 days	75 days
Trade payables payment period	45 days	42 days
Working capital cycle	54 days	

(b) Tick the one correct observation about each aspect of the business performance below.

(10 Marks)

(i) Profitability

This year, profitability has improved throughout the business. Higher sales have been the cause of this improvement.	
This year, reductions in profit, caused by higher sales at lower margins, have been successfully mitigated by careful management of overheads.	
Some profitability ratios have improved and some have deteriorated. Further investigation is required to understand whether overall profitability has improved this year.	

(ii) Financial position

The business is more financially risky as gearing has increased due to higher loans.	
Gearing has improved due to the repayment of loans in 20-5, which will reduce interest charges, improving retained profits.	
Gearing has improved in 20-5, primarily due to the profits earned and retained in 20-5. The business is now less financially risky.	

(iii) Liquidity

ABL has high levels of liquidity, so is very solvent.	
ABL has levels of liquidity that are very high. The money tied up in cash and trade receivables should be used elsewhere in the business.	
The liquidity ratio indicates the business may face problems paying its debts as they fall due.	

(iv) Working capital management

The working capital cycle ratio indicates working capital management has deteriorated, as it is too high. The additional credit offered to customers during 20-5 has contributed to this.	
The components of the working capital cycle are fairly constant. The trade receivables collection period has improved slightly and the trade payables payment period has deteriorated a little.	
Working capital management has improved, as customers are paying ABL more quickly and suppliers are offering more credit.	

(v) Overall performance

The reduction in gearing, coupled with the increase in the quick ratio, indicates an overall decline in performance.	
The improvement in the return on capital employed is solely due to the reduction in gearing. Management of working capital has improved.	
The growth in the return on capital employed indicates an overall improvement in performance.	

Task 5: 20 marks

Tim Chandler, the Accounts Assistant, is studying AAT and has commented that ABL runs it operations in a centralised manner. He would like to know if the following statements about a centralised structure are true or false.

(a) Identify whether each of the following statements about a centralised structure is true or false

Statement	**True/False**
Decision making will be faster, as the length of the scalar chain is shorter	× T
The span of control is likely to be narrower	✓ T
Productivity will be higher due to centralisation	× F
A centralised structure is more expensive to operate	× F
Branch managers will make more decisions under a centralised structure	✓ F

2 ~~(5 marks)~~

You have been asked to review ABL's purchasing procedures and to make recommendations for improvement.

Purchasing procedures:

Capital expenditure

ABL's Purchasing Manager is responsible for negotiating all new orders for capital items such as vehicles and equipment. Orders over £1,000 need to be countersigned by one of the directors.

The company has a purchase order module in its accounting software which automatically numbers all orders issued and which allows deliveries to be matched against purchase orders by the stores department and then transmitted to the Payables Ledger Clerk who matches the received orders against invoices, checks them, and then passes them for payment.

Plumbing and heating systems and supplies, including microgeneration systems

Parts are ordered by engineers, who email the supplier and charge the cost to the relevant job on Userve. Userve does not have a purchase order module but the Payables Ledger Clerk at head office who receives the invoices can check them against quoted prices that have been recorded on Userve. Over the years engineers have built up good relationships with local suppliers and will order from them.

Sometimes, the information entered onto Userve is incorrect. This has led to underpayments to suppliers, as the Payables Clerk has paid the lower amount, or delays in paying suppliers, as the engineers do not automatically send the email with agreed prices to the accounts department.

Userve has informed ABL of a new purchase order add-on for the system, costing £2,000. This could link to the accounts system and be used for ordering parts, using unique purchase order numbers, which could be matched to delivery notes and invoices.

Quotes for micro-generation systems, such as solar panels, are currently prepared by one engineer, Steve, who travels around the country. He is due to train several of the branch managers in how to quote for these systems, as they currently only know how to fit them. For customers to claim government subsidies, the systems have to be compliant with all relevant legislation. Due to the volume of quotes, Steve is travelling long distances, and has made a few errors which have resulted in ABL having to compensate customers for lost subsidies. The non-compliance issue has not been reported to the relevant regulatory body, which could penalise ABL if it finds out about this.

Fuel

The company has an account with BP. Engineers can fill up company vans at BP garages and sign for the fuel on the head office account. BP garages use a number plate recognition system so only company vehicles can be refuelled. Head office is sent monthly statements by BP, along with a detailed breakdown of fuel usage by vehicle, which ABL uses to monitor mileage costs.

Utilities and office supplies

ABL's Purchasing Manager is responsible for negotiating all remaining revenue items using the purchase order system for capital expenditure. The Purchasing Manager is very experienced and has worked for ABL for many years, working closely with the main suppliers for several years. He has recently offered to start training another staff member, as he is due to retire next year.

(b) Prepare a SWOT analysis of the purchases procedures of ABL, identifying two factors for each element.

(i) Strengths

• orders over £1k need to be countersigned by a director. More secure that only nessesiter are ordered • Account with BP. Very accurate on how much all drivers use fuel on each journey so more accurate. No personal miles.

(ii) Weaknesses

• No purchase order module and orders are done by email. No trace of a order, could forget or end up receiving the wrong item. • only one person knows how to negotiate all remaining revenue. if ~~any~~ they are ill there is ~~no one who can take over~~.

(iii) Opportunities

• purchasing manager can train someone else or a few more people.

(iv) Threats

(8 marks)

(c) **(i)** Recommend two improvements to the current payroll system. (2 marks)

(ii) Identify two benefits that each improvement would bring to the purchases system. (4 marks)

Recommendation	**Benefit**
1	**1** **2**
1	**1** **2**

(d) Identify one ethical issue currently faced by ABL.

(1 mark)

Practice synoptic assessment 2

Pre-release material

Company background and history

CD Malt Ltd (CDM) is a manufacturer of malted grains and malted products mainly for sale to the brewing industry in the UK. Originally founded in Victorian times, as a small Lincolnshire firm selling purely to brewers in Lincoln, it grew over the years and subsequently merged with a Southampton-based operation. In the 1990s it was bought by an American conglomerate. The US-based parent company has recently experienced financial problems which have led to the decision in the last year to look for a buyer for CDM. Consequently, the UK directors of CDM raised the finance necessary for a management buyout of the business which was completed at the end of the last financial year.

CDM operates from an industrial site in Lincolnshire close to the area in which the grains are grown, with a second manufacturing facility in Southampton. The Lincolnshire site accounts for approximately 2/3 of its production of malted products each year. The firm's business is seasonal; grains need to be purchased at, or shortly after, harvest time, and are then stored until required for production. This has an impact on cash flow.

Draft accounts for the year just ended show revenue of £25 million and a profit for the year of £0.8 million. The company employs 120 FTE employees, 100 of whom work in production and delivery, and the remainder in administration.

Mission statement

To obtain the best quality grains and use them to produce the best quality malt and malted products, and to provide our customers with the highest standards of service.

We aim to benefit shareholders, staff, and the communities in which we work, whilst operating ethically and sustainably.

Developments in the market

Beer sales in the UK have been in decline for many years resulting in reducing demand for malt. The company has a limited range of products, so has maintained revenue by moving into the growing market for micro-breweries and craft breweries. This has been boosted by increased sales of malt to the EU and developing economies such as India and Thailand. The market for whisky remains strong, and long-term growth is predicted for the production of malts for distilling.

Strategic planning – balanced scorecard

As part of the management buyout process, the managers assessed the underlying business using the balanced scorecard. An updated version of this for the recent draft financial results is shown below:

Learning and growth

CDM focuses on this perspective in three ways. Firstly, staff on its product development team are experienced, well qualified and committed. Secondly, the firm is committed to staff training and development with staff at all levels encouraged to undertake relevant training; this is combined with recruitment processes that ensure high calibre, new employees are engaged. Thirdly, the firm is committed to opening channels of communication from "shop floor" employees to management. This is to ensure that insights from those carrying out the work are fed into future company development.

Business processes

In the last two years, the Lincolnshire production site benefitted from updating and upgrading of production facilities. This improved its ability to produce the finest grade malts of a consistent quality, at the same time as improving its carbon footprint through improved heat reclamation in the drying process (kilning). The production facility at Southampton needs similar levels of investment to improve production quality and consistency. Production at both locations has quality accreditations including ISO9001 and Assured UK Malt (AUKM).

Customers

Customers range from multi-national breweries that buy malt by the tonne, to small micro-breweries that buy 25 kg sacks of malt. CDM works hard getting to know its customers and to provide a high standard of service. As a result it has a stable customer base. Sales have grown by 4% over the last year and customer satisfaction surveys have provided positive feedback.

Financial

Revenue growth combined with improved efficiencies at the firm's largest production site have combined to bring a 20% increase to the firm's operating profit. The firm's return on capital employed is 13.5%, up from 12.1% a year ago. The biggest challenge faced from the financial perspective relates to funding. The directors have financed the management buyout with borrowings, and it is unlikely that they will be able to obtain significant amounts of additional finance in the short term.

Management focus

Despite the strong position illustrated by the balanced scorecard, the firm continues to face many short-term challenges as it begins to operate independently. The conglomerate operated as a number of divisions with CDM's sales and production having separate reporting lines across the group. Management reporting structures now need to be redeveloped to support CDM operating as a single entity. CDM has been using systems software developed to suit the group structure and is now in the process of implementing the installation of new software across all areas of operations. The implementation outline is as follows:

Month 1: Administration, General ledger, Invoicing and Receivables ledger

Month 2: Payables ledger, Human Resources (and payroll), Inventory

Month 3: Manufacturing, Sales order processing, Purchase order processing

Staff

CDM's shareholders and directors are:

Managing Director	Simon Grainger
Production Director	Paul Arnold
Sales Director	Deborah Jones
Finance Director	Oliver Matthews
Human Resources Director	Jayne McDonald

The Southampton site is run by its Production Manager, Mark Widacombe.

The FD is in charge of the treasury aspects of the firm, including negotiating loans and forward contracts to protect the company from commodity price fluctuations, as well as fluctuations in foreign exchange rates. He is also responsible for the Accounts Department, a team of seven comprising the following:

- Management Accountant who is responsible for budgeting and costing as well as ad hoc analysis and reports
- Financial Accountant who is responsible for the production of the annual statutory accounts, the monthly management accounts and for overseeing transaction processing
- Assistant Accountant who is responsible for processing transactions, credit control, VAT returns, monitoring the bank account and month end adjustments, and who supervises the clerks
- Receivables Ledger Clerk
- Payables Ledger Clerk
- Payroll Clerk
- Temporary Accounts Assistant

CDM's financial statements are show below:

CD Malt Ltd Statement of profit or loss for the year ended 31.12.20-6

Continuing operations	£000
Revenue	25,124
Cost of sales	19,597
Gross profit	5,527
Operating expenses	3,248
Operating profit	2,279
Finance costs	1,294
Profit before tax	985
Tax	216
Profit for the period from continuing operations	**769**

CD Malt Ltd Statement of financial position as at 31.12.20-6

	£000
Assets	
Non-Current assets	
Plant property and equipment	13,444
Current assets	
Inventories	6,127
Trade receivables	3,411
Cash and cash equivalent	23
	23,005
Equities and liabilities	
Ordinary share capital (£1 shares)	300
Retained earnings	6,472
Non-current liabilities	
Debenture loans	9,200
Pension liabilities	950
Current liabilities	
Trade payables	5,966
Taxation	117
	23,005

INSTRUCTIONS

The Practice Assessment contains five tasks and you should attempt to complete every task.

Read every task carefully to make sure you understand what is required.

Where the date is relevant, it is given in the task data.

Both minus signs and brackets can be used to indicate negative numbers unless task instructions state otherwise.

You must use a full stop to indicate a decimal point. For example, write 100.57, not 100,57 or 100 57.

You may use a comma to indicate a number in the thousands, but you don't have to. For example, 10000 and 10,000 are both acceptable.

You have three hours to complete the Practice Assessment.

TASKS

Task 1: 20 marks

(a) Now that CD Malt Ltd is operating as an independent company, which regulations will it need to comply with when it prepares its year-end accounts? Tick all that apply.

Regulations		**Applies**
(a)	Companies Act 2006	✓
(b)	Sarbanes–Oxley (2002)	
(c)	London Stock Exchange regulations	
(d)	Accounting standards	✓
(e)	Financial Conduct Authority regulations	✓

(4 marks)

(b) The Accounts Assistant has been employed on a temporary basis to assist with transaction processing while the business transitions to the new IT systems. Before completing any tasks, the Accounts Assistant is required to read the procedure notes for that task and their work is then monitored by the relevant clerk. These arrangements demonstrate:

(a)	Strong personnel controls	✓
(b)	Good segregation of duties	
(c)	Strong physical controls	
(d)	Strong organisational controls	

(2 marks)

(c) Mark Widacombe, the Production Manager at Southampton, phones to report that a member of staff has left. Who would be the most appropriate person for him to talk to?

(a)	The Payroll Clerk	
(b)	The Financial Accountant	
(c)	The Finance Director	
(d)	The Human Resources Director	✓

(2 marks)

(d) The Accounts Assistant usually reconciles the cash in the tin and the petty cash vouchers to the amount at the start of the month. Identify whether the following errors and discrepancies would be detected by this reconciliation.

Error or discrepancy		**Would be detected**	**Would not be detected**
(a)	Miscoding of a petty cash voucher as travel rather than subsistence	✓	
(b)	Theft of cash from the petty cash tin	✓	
(c)	Petty cash claims have been paid for more than the maximum amount allowed	✓	
(d)	Addition error on petty cash voucher		✓
(e)	Clerical error resulting in the wrong amount of petty cash being paid out		✓

(5 marks)

(e) Identify one of the following five IT system controls that will help to protect accounting data from each of the following two issues:

(1) Human error

(2) Power failure

IT system control		**Human error**	**Power failure**
(a)	Audit trails showing all transactions posted and who posted them	✓	
(b)	Individual user-names and passwords for all users	✓	
(c)	Automatic back-ups		✓
(d)	A firewall that filters incoming email and destroys suspect items		✓
(e)	Sense checks which prevent the posting of transactions dated outside the current period	✓	

(4 marks)

(f) The whole accounts team are extremely busy during month 1 with the introduction of the new IT systems for the General ledger and Receivables ledger. As a result, despite having no previous payroll experience, the Payables Ledger Clerk has been asked to assist the Payroll Clerk, who has been unwell and is behind with processing payroll.

Which **one** of the fundamental accounting principles is most threatened by this situation?

Professional competence & due care.

Select one from: Professional behaviour, Professional competence and due care, Confidentiality, Integrity and Objectivity.

(1 mark)

(g) Identify the action the Payables Ledger Clerk should take.

(a)	Do not tell the Payroll Clerk of their lack of experience, and do any work required	
(b)	Decline to help the Payroll Clerk	
(c)	Ensure any work performed is supervised and reviewed by the Payroll Clerk	✓

(2 marks)

Task 2: 20 marks

The temporary Accounts Assistant, who is studying AAT, is currently studying internal controls. She has asked you to review the following internal controls to see if they are suitable for the purpose given.

(a) Identify whether the following internal controls are suitable for the purpose given.

Internal control	**Purpose**	**Suitable Yes / No**
Regularly reconcile the VAT control account	Prevent and detect fraud and error	
The directors are the only authorised signatories on the bank accounts	Compliance	
The new accounting system is cloud based and is backed up automatically	Facilitate operations	

(3 marks)

CDM's customers usually buy on credit, but some customers buy in cash direct from the warehouse. You have been asked by Deborah Jones, the Sales Director, whether the following controls in a sales ordering system are appropriate for cash-based or credit-based transactions.

(b) Identify whether the following controls are more suitable for cash-based or credit-based transactions.

Internal control	**Cash-based**	**Credit-based**
Customers are subject to rigorous credit checks with a credit agency prior to orders being placed		
Customers pay for the goods at the point of order and collection		

(2 marks)

You have been asked to carry out a review of CDM's proposed Receivables ledger procedures which are outlined below.

In month 1 the Invoicing and Receivables ledger module of the new IT system goes live. However, the Sales Order Processing module which will link to it does not go live until month 3. As a result, temporary procedures have been introduced to be used for the interim period where there will be no automatic updates to the accounting system from the sales team or despatch departments.

Ordering and despatch

- Sales staff will be responsible for pricing customer orders received using a spreadsheet produced for that purpose. A separate worksheet will be used for each order. Sales staff will be able to view customer accounts on the IT system and will check their current status and credit limits before accepting orders.
- Once an order is accepted, the sales staff will print a copy of the worksheet and email it to the customer. They will also email a copy of the worksheet to the production department and to the Receivables Ledger Clerk.
- Production schedules will be planned around customer orders, and once goods are ready for shipping, the order worksheets will be emailed to the despatch department. Once goods have been despatched, the worksheet is updated to show despatch details and the updated worksheet will be emailed to the Receivables Ledger Clerk.

Accounting

- The Receivables Ledger Clerk must raise invoices on the basis of worksheets received from despatch. These will be priced automatically by the new software, including VAT where appropriate, and will state the agreed terms of sale. These sheets will then be emailed to customers.
- Customer queries relating to orders and receipts are initially directed to the sales team. If a credit note is required to resolve an issue, the Sales Manager will email the Receivables Ledger Clerk asking for a credit note to be raised and explaining why this is necessary.
- Customer statements are produced at the month end on the new software and then emailed to customers.
- The Assistant Accountant will reconcile the total of the receivables ledger balances to the receivables ledger control account at the month end.

(c) Using the table on the next page:

(i) Identify FIVE systemic weaknesses in CDM's proposed procedures, including its internal controls, that underpin the sales accounting.

(5 marks)

(ii) Explain how each weakness you have identified could create a problem for the company.

(10 marks)

Weakness	Potential problem for the company
Weakness 1	
Weakness 2	
Weakness 3	
Weakness 4	
Weakness 5	

Task 3: 20 marks

(a) Deborah Jones, the Sales Director, wants to develop a new malt for a lighter beer, to meet demand for a new trend in the beer market. To determine a suitable price for the new malt, she has asked you to help her cost the product. She wants to use life cycle costing which looks at the costs of the whole product. Deborah has not used life cycle costing before and would like you to clarify her understanding of it.

Identify if each of the following statements about a product life cycle and life cycle costing is true or false.

Statement	**True / False**
Revenues are likely to be highest in the growth stage of the product	
The learning effect is likely to reduce costs in the growth and maturity stages	
The majority of costs will be fixed in the development stage	
Higher automation costs should only be incurred if production costs fall as a result	
Marketing costs will continue to be high in the maturity stage	

(5 marks)

(b) The Southampton plant processes two grades of barley to produce malt. Grade A is used for beer and grade B is used for whisky. Malting processes are identical for the two grades. Costs and revenues are as follows:

	Grade A Barley	**Grade B Barley**
Raw materials cost	£180 per tonne	£160 per tonne
Other manufacturing costs	£25 per tonne	£25 per tonne
Malt selling price	£250 per tonne	£225 per tonne

A machine breakdown at Southampton means that there will not be enough processing time this month to complete all the orders that have been scheduled.

Paul Arnold, the Production Director, wants to know the order to produce each product.

(i) For each product calculate the variable cost and contribution per tonne.

	Grade A barley	**Grade B barley**
Variable cost per tonne, £		
Contribution per tonne, £		

(4 marks)

(ii) Select the order the products should be produced in.

Select from: First, Second

Product	**Production**
Grade A barley	
Grade B barley	

(2 marks)

(iii) Identify practical steps which could be taken to reduce the impact of the machine breakdown.

(5 marks)

(iv) Identify four other factors CDM should consider when choosing to prioritise production of one grade of barley over another and taking the steps in part (iii).

(4 marks)

Task 4: 20 marks

(a) Use the extracts of the financial statements shown below to complete the calculation of financial ratios shown on the next page.

(10 marks)

CD Malt Ltd Statement of profit or loss	**Year ended 30.12.20-5**	**Year ended 30.12.20-6**
	£000	£000
Revenue	24,158	25,124
Gross profit	5,073	5,527
Operating profit	1,895	2,279
Profit before tax	1,066	985
CD Malt Ltd Statement of financial position		
Assets		
Non-current assets	12,841	13,444
Inventories	5,890	6,127
Trade receivables	3,282	3,411
Cash and cash equivalents	158	23
Current assets	9,330	9,561
Total assets	**22,171**	**23,005**
Equities and liabilities		
Equity	10,087	6,772
Non-current liabilities	5,574	10,150
Trade payables	6,398	5,966
Taxation	112	117
Current liabilities	6,510	6,083
Total equity and liabilities	**22,171**	**23,005**

Ratios

Show profitability, financial position, and liquidity ratios to one decimal place. Working capital ratios should be rounded to the nearest day.

Complete the shaded boxes.

Ratio	Year ended 30.12.20-5	Year ended 30.12.20-6
Profitability		
Gross profit margin %	21.0%	22.0%
Operating profit margin %	7.8%	
Return on capital employed	12.1%	13.5%
Financial position		
Interest cover	2.3 times	
Gearing	35.6%	
Liquidity		
Current ratio	1.4:1	
Quick/acid test ratio	0.5:1	0.6:1
Working capital management		
Inventory holding period	113 days	114 days
Trade receivables collection period	50 days	50 days
Trade payables payment period	122 days	

(b) Select the most appropriate observation about each aspect of the business's performance.

(10 Marks)

Profitability

(a)	The business has generated more profits in 20-6 than in 20-5	
(b)	Growth in sales volumes has caused an increase in the gross profit margin which has caused an increase in the operating profit margin	
(c)	The improvement in the gross profit margin and the operating profit margin could not have been achieved if costs had increased in line with revenue	

Financial position

(a)	The business has gone from having low levels of gearing in 20-5 to medium levels of gearing in 20-6	
(b)	The interest cover is healthy, but the level of gearing gives cause for concern	
(c)	The company has gone from having medium levels of gearing in 20-5 to high levels of gearing in 20-6	

Liquidity

(a)	Both liquidity ratios have improved over the year	
(b)	The changes in the ratios are too small to enable meaningful interpretation of the data	
(c)	Both ratios are a cause for concern as the current ratio should not fall below 2:1 and the acid test ratio should not fall below 1:1	

Working capital management

(a)	The working capital cycle has improved by 12 days	
(b)	From the perspective of a supplier to CRM, the change in the trade payables payment period is a deterioration	
(c)	The change in the trade payables payment period indicates a lack of financial control	

Overall performance

(a)	20-6 has been a good year, sales growth has driven growth in profits and there has only been a moderate increase in gearing	
(b)	Although underlying profitability has improved in 20-6, the level of gearing and resultant interest costs are a significant cause for concern	
(c)	Both underlying profitability and the level of gearing have increased in 20-6; gearing is not an issue as the interest cover remains good	

Task 5: 20 marks

Some products CDM produces undergo several processes before they can be sold. Some local businesses can supply products that have been part-processed, which CDM could buy and complete the processing. Paul Arnold, the Production Director, has suggested CDM considers doing this to improve profitability.

(a) Identify whether each of the following statements is true or false regarding this decision.

Statement	**True**	**False**
Only relevant costs should be included in the make or buy decision		
The quality of the bought-in product will always be as good as what CDM can produce		
The reliability of supply should be considered as part of the decision-making process		
Production overheads currently absorbed into CDM's partly-processed products should be included in the cost comparison of making or buying the product		
The only consideration in the decision should be financial		

(5 marks)

You have been asked to review a new forecasting system for planning grain purchases. The current system operates as follows:

Current Grain Purchase forecasting and planning procedures

Deborah Jones and Paul Arnold, the Sales and Production Directors, respectively, meet in the run up to harvest to calculate the expected sales volumes for the coming year by category of malt. This will feed into plans for the quantity to be purchased. Oliver Matthews, the Finance Director, gets involved at this point as he will need to make sure that the business can finance the level of purchases required.

Once plans are agreed, CDM's two buyers will be informed, and they will work together to achieve the planned levels of purchases. To improve the reliability and quality of supplies, CDM agrees long-term contracts with farmers who sell the grains. These contracts are at a fixed price for three years - CDM gets guaranteed supply, and the farmers get a guaranteed price, dependant on quality. Approximately 50% of required purchases are covered by these agreements. The remainder is bought on the open market and may sometimes be imported if required, although this is usually more expensive.

New Grain Purchase forecasting and planning system

You have been investigating several software packages to help with grain forecasting and have identified some suitable new software, GrainStore. The research costs to date have been £3,600. The existing grain contracts would need to be loaded into the new system, at a cost of £6,000.

If the system is purchased, Deborah Jones, Paul Arnold and Oliver Matthews would all need to attend a two-day training course, costing £1,600 per person. You would also need to attend the course. The two buyers would need to attend a one-day course costing £800 each.

The software licence costs £15,000 per annum and some hardware upgrades costing £17,500 would be required.

This year, CDM expects to purchase grain costing £12.4 million. Improving the forecasting and buying of grain as a result of the new system is expected to save 0.5% of the total grain costs. Overtime totalling £3,000 per year, currently paid to the buyers, will also be saved. The buyers have received this payment for several years.

The new system would be able to provide much more extensive reporting of information than the current system.

(b) **(i)** Complete a financial cost-benefit analysis for the proposed forecasting and planning system, GrainStore, stating if it is a net cost or benefit.

Costs	£
Benefits	
(Net cost)/benefit	

(6 marks)

(ii) Identify six non-financial factors that should be considered as part of the cost-benefit analysis.

(6 marks)

(iii) Recommend, with two reasons, whether or not the proposed investment should be made.

(3 marks)

Practice synoptic assessment 3

Pre-release material

Company background and history

The Fabled Baker Limited (FBL) is a food manufacturer that runs a chain of bakeries operating in the Midlands. The company owns a factory where it produces the majority of the items sold in its shops. The company's head office is based at its factory on an industrial estate in Coventry.

The company was started by master baker Peter Taylor and his wife Jean who set up a single bakers' shop in Tamworth in the 1960s. The firm expanded over the years and by the late 1980s had become a limited company owned and managed by the Taylor family with over 80 high street shops, all with instore bakeries. At this point the factory was built, and all instore bakeries were closed. The management of the firm moved to Coventry and consolidated operations as a regional bakery network. Over the next 10 years, the Taylor family became less active in the management of the company.

The firm continued to expand until the start of the recession in 20-4. Margins had always been tight due to supermarket competition, but this had been offset by sales volume. However, sales volumes fell dramatically in 20-4. Management's response was to close some shops and to focus on the 'food-on-the-go' market. This move has seen the company return to profitability. The majority of shares in FBL are now owned by the Taylor family, together with the current Sales, Production and Finance Directors, who each have a 10% stake in the company.

In 20-6 FBL had revenue of £42 million, an increase of 3% compared with 20-5. It has 73 shops and employs 924 employees, 675 working in the shops, 210 in the factory and distribution, and the remainder in Product Development, Administration and Finance.

Mission statement

The Fabled Baker Limited aims to live up to its name, providing high quality and memorable food to all its customers with outstanding levels of customer service.

The firm is, at its core, a family business deeply rooted in the Midlands with a strong work ethic and strong commitment to staff, customers, and local communities.

Developments in the market

There is a continued trend in declining sales of traditional bakery products such as loaves of bread. However, alongside this there is significant growth in the market for 'food-on-the-go'. Demand for sandwiches, savouries such as sausage rolls and pasties, as well as biscuits and cakes, continues to grow. FBL has recently developed a number of new products, such as a breakfast range, and a range of fresh soups. The soups have been so successful that in 20-6 FBL has supplied them to four supermarket chains for sale in their chilled food sections. The credit sales of soup accounted for 3% of total sales in 20-6. FBL has also invested in coffee machines for its shops and opened a small number of new 'out of town' shops in areas it has identified as having few shops, but where many people work.

Several high streets and town centres continue to struggle with the changing demand caused by out-of-town shopping centres and the increase in online shopping. FBL has several stores that are generating very low profits.

FBL has always paid its staff above the minimum wage, and staff costs for 20-6 rose by 5% as wage rates were increased to maintain pay differentials. The prices of raw materials also rose, partly as a result of a rise in the minimum wage, and partly because Britain left the European Union (Brexit).

Strategic planning and control

The company reviews four key areas to assess its overall performance.

Learning and growth

FBL employs a well-qualified product development team at its factory. They are responsible for constantly reviewing and renewing the firm's product range in line with changing consumer tastes. In 20-6 20% of product lines were "refreshed" and like-for-like sales responded with growth of 8%. In addition, 56 new products were added to the firm's product portfolio over the year. In week 52, 12% of sales came from product lines launched in 20-6. Training requirements of established and new staff are carefully reviewed, and staff regularly attend training sessions at head office such as how to operate the barista coffee machines that have been installed in the shops.

Business processes

In 20-5, the firm upgraded one production line at its factory and invested in a new soup-making production facility. This investment, along with the refurbishment of eight shops and the investment in new equipment at all shops, has increased the capacity of the firm to meet its customers' needs.

Customers

Customer satisfaction is monitored through performance indicators, measuring both footfall and average spend per customer in each shop. Both indicators showed positive growth in 20-6. In addition, regular customer satisfaction surveys are carried out. At the end of 20-6, these show that FBL's customers see the business as offering high quality products that are good value for money and provided with a friendly service.

Financial

Revenue grew by 3% in 20-6, and the firm achieved a ROCE of 13%, up from 12% in 20-5. The Taylor family is pleased with this improvement, but the other directors are keen to see the company further improve its financial results. They argue that because of the general level of economic uncertainty, FBL needs to base more of its decisions on purely financial factors. In particular, it must seriously consider whether to close or re-develop marginally profitable shops.

Staff

FBL's key personnel are:

Managing Director	Robert Taylor
Production Director	Brian Stead
Sales Director	Elaine Anderson
Finance Director	Alison Davis
Human Resources Director	Sanjeev Grover
Management Accountant	Joy Patel
Assistant Accountant	Kris Lewinski
Financial Accountant	Hannah Cobb
Accounts Payable Clerk	Jim Pickwick
Payroll & Accounts Receivable Clerk	Naomi Berne

Alison Davis, the Finance Director, produces FBL's annual statutory accounts and is responsible for all finance, legal and IT issues.

Joy Patel, the Management Accountant, is responsible for the standard costing system, the monthly management accounts, and the annual budgets. Hannah Cobb, the Financial Accountant is responsible for the day-to-day running of the transaction processing systems.

FBL's financial statements for 20-6 are shown below.

The Fabled Baker Limited Statement of profit or loss for the year ended 31.12.20-6

Continuing operations	**£000**
Revenue	41,800
Cost of sales	25,916
Gross profit	15,884
Operating expenses	14,667
Operating profit	1,217
Finance costs	41
Profit before tax	1,176
Tax	259
Profit for the period from continuing operations	917

The Fabled Baker Limited Statement of financial position as at 31.12.20-6

	£000
Assets	
Non-Current assets	
Plant property and equipment	11,296
Current assets	
Inventories	1,136
Trade receivables	309
Cash and cash equivalents	61
Total assets	12,802
Equities and liabilities	
Ordinary share capital (£1 shares)	2,000
Retained earnings	6,525
Total equity	8,525
Non-current liabilities	
Loans	510
Current liabilities	
Trade payables	3,560
Taxation	207
Total liabilities	4,277
Total equity and liabilities	12,802

INSTRUCTIONS

The Practice Assessment contains five tasks and you should attempt to complete every task.

Read every task carefully to make sure you understand what is required.

Where the date is relevant, it is given in the task data.

Both minus signs and brackets can be used to indicate negative numbers unless task instructions state otherwise.

You must use a full stop to indicate a decimal point. For example, write 100.57, not 100,57 or 100 57.

You may use a comma to indicate a number in the thousands, but you don't have to. For example, 10000 and 10,000 are both acceptable.

You have three hours to complete the Practice Assessment

TASKS

Task 1: 20 marks

(a) Link each of the stakeholders to valid reasons for their interest in the annual statutory accounts of a company.

	Lenders	Credit customers	Shareholders
To assess potential for future growth			
To assess security for borrowings			
To assess potential for future dividend payments			

(3 marks)

(b) At FBL, Naomi Berne, the Payroll and Accounts Receivable Clerk, is responsible for issuing sales invoices and statements to credit customers; Jim Pickwick, the Accounts Payable Clerk, is responsible for issuing credit notes to customers; and Kris Lewinski, the Assistant Accountant, records receipts from customers.

When producing the list of aged receivables for the monthly management accounts, Joy Patel, the Management Accountant, notices that one credit note has not been correctly allocated against an invoice.

Which is the most appropriate course of action for the Joy to take?

(a)	Log on to the accounting system and match the credit note	
(b)	Advise Jim Pickwick, the Accounts Payable clerk, of the error so that it can be rectified	
(c)	Advise Kris Lewinski, the Assistant Accountant, of the error so that it can be rectified	
(d)	Do nothing as the balance on the account is correct	

(2 marks)

(c) Monthly rolling inventory counts of inventory held at FBL's factory are carried out. Kris Lewinski, the Assistant Accountant, is required to reconcile the inventory counted to the inventory records, to detect errors that have occurred. She has identified that the amount of material FG442 counted is lower than the inventory records show.

Identify whether each of these situations could have caused the error that has been detected by the reconciliation between the physical inventory count and the inventory records for FG442.

Situation		**Would result in the error that has been detected**	**Would not result in the error that has been detected**
(a)	Receipt of goods incorrectly recorded as 100 units instead of 1,000 units		
(b)	Theft of items from stores		
(c)	An issue from stores to production incorrectly recorded as 100 units instead of 1,000 units		
(d)	A container of goods on the production line was counted twice		
(e)	Inventory records not updated for disposal of out-of-date inventory		

(5 marks)

(d) Identify which of the controls below will prevent, rather than detect, errors.

(a)	Bank reconciliation	
(b)	Accounting system will not accept transactions with a date in the future	
(c)	Analysis of costs by department and investigation of variances in the monthly management accounts	
(d)	Users only have access to the parts of the system required for their job	
(e)	Credit notes need to be raised by one of the clerks and checked by Hannah Cobb, the Financial Accountant, before they are approved for posting	
(f)	Audit trails show which user posted each transaction	
(g)	Journals are entered by qualified accounts personnel	

(4 marks)

(e) At the year-end, the balance of cash at bank has dipped significantly lower than planned. Jamie Taylor, the Production Manager, suggests that you keep the cash book open for a couple of days to capture more cash receipts from the shops and boost the bank balance. This will give a false picture of the cash position in the financial statements.

Which **one** ethical principle is most threatened by this suggestion?

Select from: Professional behaviour, Professional competence and due care, Confidentiality, Integrity, and Objectivity.

(2 marks)

(f) How should you respond to Jamie's suggestion?

Select the correct option.

Response	
Agree that this is a good idea as it is good for FBL's financial statements	
Close the cash book as normal	
Ask Robert Taylor, the Managing Director, what he would prefer to do, as he signs the financial statements	

(2 marks)

(g) Trudi Taylor, one of the Regional Sales Managers, has been investigating the amounts of unsold food in shops at the end of each day and whether or not it can be given to charities, such as soup kitchens. She asks for support from the Finance Director, Alison Davis, and says that she has an ethical duty as an accountant to support sustainability.

Identify whether this statement is true or false.

(2 marks)

Task 2: 20 marks

(a) You have been helping Naomi Berne, the Payroll & Accounts Receivable Clerk, to understand internal controls. She has asked you to help her categorise the following controls.

Select from the following options: Segregation, Organisational, Authorisation, Personnel, Supervision, Physical, Arithmetic & Accounting, Management.

Description	Internal control
(a) Ensuring employees have appropriate qualifications for their job	
(b) Credit notes are raised by the Accounts Payable Clerk and signed off by the Financial Accountant	
(c) Variances between actual and budget are investigated each month	
(d) Supplier statements are regularly reconciled with the payables ledger	
(e) Vehicle registration documents are kept in a locked cabinet in the Finance Director's office	

(5 marks)

(b) You have been asked to review the controls in the credit sales system at FBL and have established the following.

Background

- FBL's sales team deal with shop products and promotions, rather than credit sales.
- The Product Development Manager deals with supermarkets and negotiating sales with them.
- There are currently four credit customers, all of whom have deliveries on a daily basis to their regional distribution centres. Several new customers are expected to start buying from FBL next month.

Ordering and delivery

- Purchase orders from the supermarkets are emailed to the Product Development Manager who uses the accounting system's sales order processing module to record them and communicate the orders to the Production Manager.
- Once production is complete, despatch notes are produced from the accounting software and a hard copy is given to the delivery driver who will get the customer's signature for receipt of the goods.
- The signed despatch notes are returned to Naomi Berne, the Payroll and Accounts Receivable Clerk, who then uses the accounting software to raise sales invoices which are posted to customers.

Recording receipts and account management

- The supermarkets pay by BACS on 90 day terms.
- The accounting software used by FBL has a receivables ledger module which is integrated with the general ledger and with the sales order processing module. Invoices raised automatically update customers' accounts.
- Kris Lewinski, the Assistant Accountant, downloads a bank statement on a daily basis and updates ledgers for receipts. Should there be a dispute with a customer about the quality or quantity of a delivery, it is investigated by Jim Pickwick, the Accounts Payable Clerk, who will produce credit notes as required.
- Credit notes need authorisation by Hannah Cobb, the Financial Accountant, and once authorisation has been obtained, they are posted to the customers' accounts.
- Statements are sent to customers on a monthly basis by Naomi Berne. An aged receivables report is included in the monthly management accounts.

(i) Using the table on the next page, identify FIVE systemic weaknesses with FBL's procedures, including its internal controls, that underpin its accounting for credit sales.

(5 marks)

(ii) For each weakness you have identified, explain how it could create a problem for the company. (10 marks)

Weakness	Potential problem for the company
Weakness 1	
Weakness 2	
Weakness 3	
Weakness 4	
Weakness 5	

Task 3: 20 marks

One of the directors at FBL has suggested outsourcing some of its products when demand is particularly high.

(a) Identify whether each of the following statements in relation to outsourcing or make or buy decisions is true or false.

Statement		**True**	**False**
(a)	The unit cost comparison of make or buy should only include additional costs incurred when making the product		
(b)	The only factor to consider in the make or buy decision is the unit cost per product		
(c)	Significant variations in volume could have an impact on whether to make or buy the products		
(d)	Fixed factory overheads absorbed by the products currently being made will need to be absorbed elsewhere if a business buys or outsources		
(e)	The quality of the products will always be the same, if made or outsourced		

(5 marks)

FBL uses traditional overhead absorption methods to allocate and apportion overheads to units produced. Joy Patel, the Management Accountant, is investigating the option of introducing activity-based costing and has asked you to perform some preliminary calculations for this.

£180,000 per annum that is spent on product development is included in overheads that are absorbed into production on the basis of machine hours. This includes the costs of redesigning products, test bakes, and approval and set-up for mass production.

In 20-6, the recipes for a total of 90 products were designed, or re-designed.

(b) **(i)** Calculate the activity-based costing cost driver recovery rate for product development.

£ [ ] per recipe.

(2 marks)

The 90 products designed includes sausage rolls and all of the soups produced during the year. Once the new recipe for sausage rolls was agreed, it was used all year (300 working days), but each soup recipe was only used for four weeks (24 working days).

On each working day, 7,000 sausage rolls and 1,000 litres of soup were produced.

(ii) Taking an activity-based costing approach, calculate the cost of product development in pence to two decimal places per litre of soup.

[ ] pence per litre of soup.

(2 marks)

(iii) Taking an activity-based costing approach, calculate the cost of product development in pence to two decimal places per sausage roll.

[ ] pence per sausage roll.

(2 marks)

(iv) Explain how the introduction of activity-based costing might improve decision making at FBL.

(5 marks)

(c) Identify four non-financial factors that FBL may wish to consider before making a final decision on whether to use activity-based costing.

(4 marks)

Task 4: 20 marks

Alison Davis, the Finance Director, wants to monitor how well a new out of town shop is performing compared with a typical current high street shop, and the company's overall performance. She has asked you to do some analysis of this.

(a) Use the extracts from the financial statements shown to complete the calculation of financial ratios shown below. (5 marks)

Statement of profit or loss	**Year ended 30.12.20-6**	**6 months ended 30.12.20-6**
	£000	£000
	High street shop	**New out of town shop**
	£000	£000
Revenue	389	230
Gross profit	136	90
Operating profit	4	12
Profit before tax	3	10
Statement of financial position	**31.12.20-6**	**31.12.20-6**
Assets	£000	£000
Non-current assets	43	201
Inventories	8	6
Cash and cash equivalents	1	1
	52	208
Financed by		
Non-current loan	52	208

Ratios

Show profitability ratios to two decimal places. Working capital ratios should be rounded to the nearest day.

Complete the shaded boxes.

Ratio	**Company overall**	**High street shop**	**New out of town shop**
Profitability			
Gross profit margin %	38.00%		39.13%
Operating profit margin %	2.91%	1.03%	
Asset turnover (net assets)	4.63 times		2.21 times
Return on capital employed	13.47%	7.69%	
Inventory holding period	16 days		8 days

(b) Based on the information for the company overall, the high street shop and the new out of town shop, select the correct statement about FBL's performance from those given below.

(5 marks)

(i)

The gross profit margin is worse for the new out of town shop than the high street shop	
The gross profit margin is worse for the high street shop than the new out of town shop	
The gross profit margin for the new out of town shop is better than the company's overall gross profit margin, which is a cause for concern	
If more out of town shops were opened, the company's overall gross profit margin would deteriorate, based on this information	

(ii)

The operating profit margin is worse for the new out of town shop than the high street shop	
The operating profit margin is better for the high street shop than the company overall	
The operating profit margin for the new out of town shop is better than the company's overall operating profit margin, which is a cause for concern	
If more out of town shops were opened, the company's overall operating profit margin would increase, based on this information	

(iii)

The asset turnover (net assets) for the new out of town shop may be depressed because of the value of recently purchased land and buildings	
The asset turnover (net assets) for the high street shop is better than the new out of town shop	
The asset turnover (net assets) for the new out of town shop is better than for the company overall	
Based on this shop, the asset turnover (net assets) will improve if more out of town shops are opened	

(iv)

The return on capital employed for the high street shop is better than the new out of town shop	
The return on capital employed for the company is better than the high street shop's return on capital employed	
The company's return on capital employed will improve if non-current assets are revalued up	
The return on capital employed for the new out of town shop is better than the high street shop due the high street shop having lower net assets	

(v)

The inventory holding period for the new out of town shop is worse than for the company overall	
The inventory holding periods for both shops are lower than for the company overall, as inventory is held at the factory	
The low inventory holding period for the company indicates inventory will never go out of date	
The inventory holding period for both the company and the shops is too low and should be much higher, to ensure demand is met	

(c) It is now 30 June 20-7. If you assume all the key performance indicators (KPIs) for the company overall have deteriorated, state which of the following factors could have caused them to get worse.

(10 Marks)

Choose the correct option for each KPI.

Key performance indicator	Factor causing the KPI to get worse
Gross profit margin %	Increased selling prices / Reduced selling prices / Reduced cost of goods sold
Operating profit margin %	Increased overheads / Reduced overheads / Increased finance costs
Asset turnover (net assets)	Increased revenue / Reduced revenue / Reduced net assets
Return on capital employed	Increased operating profit / Reduced capital employed / Increased capital employed
Inventory holding period	Efficient inventory management / Purchase of raw materials due to discounts offered / Reduced inventory of raw materials

Task 5: 20 marks

(a) Elaine Anderson, the Sales Director, has been on several management training courses and is keen to understand whether the internal controls over the shops in her area are suitable for the size of FBL, a large organisation.

Identify whether the following internal controls are more suitable for a small, medium, or large organisation.

Internal control	Small	Medium	Large
Exception reporting is used to investigate tills where discrepancies between cash takings and till information are higher than £5 per till, per shift			
Shop managers are responsible for compliance with food hygiene certification by staff employed in the shop			
When the Regional Sales Manager visits a shop, they review the value of wastage for the last month			
Shop managers authorise product promotions, and monitor their success			
At a specific time of day, certain products are reduced in price via the till software			

(5 marks)

(b) Staff costs make up over 40% of FBL's costs, and the biggest component of these costs relates to hourly paid shop workers, ie, all shop staff apart from the shop managers who are salaried.

You have been asked to carry out a review of FBL's payroll procedures for hourly paid shop staff, and to make recommendations for improvement. The current systems are detailed below.

Payroll procedures

Shop managers are responsible for the level of staffing in their shops. If they feel they need more staff, positions will be advertised and shop managers are responsible for interviewing and selecting new employees, passing relevant documentation to Human Resources (HR), and for arranging for new employees to attend induction training at head office.

HR records details of new starters in the payroll system. HR is also responsible for removing all leavers from the system once these have been notified by shop managers.

Shop managers all use a standard spreadsheet to plan staff shifts. Rotas are displayed in shops two weeks in advance, and the shift rota is emailed to Naomi Berne, the Payroll and Accounts Receivable Clerk, at the same time.

Staff book annual leave with their shop manager. This is recorded by the shop manager on an HR spreadsheet, and updates are sent to HR on a weekly basis. HR monitors staff holidays, sick leave, and any other staff absences.

Employees use smart cards to clock in and out of shops. At the end of each day, clocking in/out data is downloaded from the clocking terminal onto a USB stick by the shop managers and emailed to Naomi Berne for analysis and processing. Naomia Berne reviews the data and runs exception reports to check that the data is within expected parameters. High or low numbers of hours for individual staff members are checked back to the shift rotas to check their validity.

FBL uses a standard accounting software package for payroll which is RTI-compliant (UK HMRC Real Time Information). This comes with automatic updates and support provided via a telephone helpdesk. The Payroll Clerk exports the details of shop staff hours worked into the payroll system on a daily basis. She runs the monthly payroll four working days before the end of the month.

Check printouts are produced showing employee costs for each shop, as well as details for all starters and leavers. These printouts are passed to Hannah Cobb, the Financial Accountant, who spends several hours reviewing them with the Payroll Clerk.

After the payroll has been agreed, the Payroll Clerk produces a BACS transfer authority which is signed by two of the authorised signatories – these are the Financial Accountant and the directors. Staff are paid by BACS on the last working day of the month.

(b) Prepare a SWOT analysis of the payroll department of FBL, identifying two strengths, two weaknesses, two opportunities and two threats.

Strengths
Weaknesses
Opportunities
Threats

(8 marks)

(c) **(i)** Recommend two improvements to the current payroll system.

(2 marks)

(ii) Identify two benefits that each improvement would bring to the payroll system

(4 marks)

Use the table below to answer parts (i) and (ii)

Recommendations	**Benefits**

(d) Suggest one way shop managers could be trained and supported in the relevant employment laws.

(1 mark)

Practice synoptic assessment 4

Pre-release material

Company background and history

EG Products Ltd (EGP) is a manufacturer of refuse collection equipment. The main source of revenue is the sale of refuse collection vehicles, along with steel recycling banks, of the type commonly used for collection of paper and cardboard. A second stream of revenue comes from the maintenance and repair of the vehicles.

EGP has its head office on an industrial estate near Newcastle upon Tyne. The site includes production facilities and offices from which the business is managed. The company was founded in the 1980s, initially servicing a single local government sub-contractor. At that point, the firm was owner-managed; however, external equity investment was required to finance the firm's expansion and to ensure that production facilities were first class. Each of the five directors has a 10% stake in the equity of the firm; the balance of shares is held by private equity providers.

In 20-6, the company generated revenue of £18 million. It employs 135 FTE employees, 115 of whom work in production either in the factory or as field engineers. The balance are office staff working in sales and administration.

Mission statement

EGP aims to use the best raw materials for each item produced, to have production processes that ensure all output is of the highest standard, and to complete maintenance and services to the highest standards.

EGP is committed to giving customers great value for money, developing our employees, working in fair partnership with our suppliers, and promoting sustainability.

Developments in the market

There are several opposing forces affecting the size of the market in which EGP operates. Firstly, customers are either local authorities or private businesses to whom councils have sub-contracted work. Central government cuts over several years have significantly reduced the size of budgets for waste management in these organisations. As a result, vehicles are often used more intensively - for instance, by 'double-shifting' them. This could involve them being used for an early shift collecting general waste, and then a late shift collecting recycling, both on the same day. Another consequence is that the working lives of both vehicles and recycling banks are extended because these organisations will use them for longer before replacing them. Whilst this is not good news for sales of new products, EGP does benefit from increased repair and maintenance work.

A second feature of the market which is initiating change is the drive towards sustainability by UK local authorities, which have measures in place that aim to double the amount of waste recycled within 10 years.

Strategic planning

The company uses the balanced scorecard to assess its overall performance.

Learning and growth

EGP constantly invests in product development. Recent innovations include the development of new vehicles which require fewer operators (enabling savings in staff costs), the ability to install hybrid or electric engines in refuse vehicles, and options to install in-cab technology and CCTV. Twice a year, managers formally review staff performance and individual training needs to ensure that the skills of the workforce keep up with the rate of product development. This enables the company to respond flexibly to a changing market.

Business processes

EGP uses computer aided design software to ensure that all product designs are of the highest standard. Investment in production equipment, such as the laser cutting equipment and the welding robots in use, helps to ensure that the firm has the capacity to produce high quality items, and rigorous inspection and testing procedures ensure that production has achieved that level of quality. The firm continuously monitors quality issues, including production delays, customer complaints and repairs under warranty. EGP is an affiliate member of CIWM (Chartered Institute of Waste Management) and of VBRA (Vehicle Builders and Repairers Association).

Customers

EGP has an 'After-Sales Department' that manages relationships with customers while new products are under warranty and also where EGP has a maintenance or service contract with the customer. Customer satisfaction surveys are regularly completed when the customer receives a new vehicle, after workers have been trained on how to operate the vehicle, and once the vehicle is in use. Follow up calls are made by the After-Sales team to check on customer satisfaction whenever service or maintenance work has been completed. Levels of customer satisfaction are high in almost all areas, although EGP is not always as competitive on price as it would like to be. It does not have the economies of scale of some of its competitors.

Financial

In 20-6, sales volumes grew by 4% compared with 20-5. However, price competition meant that revenue only grew by 2%.

Staff

EGP's staff responsible for the overall strategy of the firm are:

Managing Director	Andrea Heppell
Production Director	Glenn MacArthur
Sales Director	Gloria Clarke
Finance Director	Martin Boyd
Human Resources Director	Narissa Sealy
Financial Accountant	Simone Hyde
Assistant Accountant (covering Cashier & Accounts Receivables)	Amy Barton
Accounts Payable Clerk	Nish Ghati
Payroll & General Ledger Clerk	Leon Novak

Date

It is early January 20-7.

EGP's financial statements for 20-6 are shown on the next page.

EG Products Ltd Statement of profit or loss for the year ended 31.12.20-6

Continuing operations	**£000**
Revenue	18,237
Cost of sales	15,137
Gross profit	3,100
Operating expenses	2,735
Operating profit	365
Finance costs	45
Profit before tax	320
Tax	64
Profit for the period from continuing operations	256

EG Products Ltd Statement of financial position as at 31.12.20-6

Assets	£000
Non-Current assets	
Plant property and equipment	654
Current assets	
Inventories	2,613
Trade receivables	2,148
Cash and cash equivalents	707
Total assets	6,122
Equities and liabilities	
Ordinary share capital (£1 shares)	2,000
Retained earnings	1,956
Total equity	3,956
Non-current liabilities	
Loans	500
Current liabilities	
Trade payables	1,617
Taxation	49
Total liabilities	2,166
Total equity and liabilities	6,122

INSTRUCTIONS

The Practice Assessment contains five tasks and you should attempt to complete every task.

Read every task carefully to make sure you understand what is required.

Where the date is relevant, it is given in the task data.

Both minus signs and brackets can be used to indicate negative numbers unless task instructions state otherwise.

You must use a full stop to indicate a decimal point. For example, write 100.57, not 100,57 or 100 57.

You may use a comma to indicate a number in the thousands, but you don't have to. For example, 10000 and 10,000 are both acceptable.

You have three hours to complete the Practice Assessment

TASKS

Task 1: 20 marks

(a) The table below shows a range of purchases-related queries. Identify which should be directed to the Accounts Department and which should be dealt with by the Purchasing team.

Departments		**Accounts Department**	**Purchasing team**
(a)	Preferred supplier for a particular purchased component		
(b)	Financial stability of a new supplier		
(c)	Agreed price lists		
(d)	Due date for payment of an invoice		

(4 marks)

(b) Identify whether each of the following should be included in a cash flow forecast.

Item		**Include in cash flow**	**Do not include in cash flow**
(a)	Forecast profit on sale of equipment		
(b)	Write off of an impaired asset		
(c)	Loan for new equipment		
(d)	Rent due from shared factory car park		

(4 marks)

(c) The Purchasing Manager asks Martin Boyd, the Finance Director, for some assistance from Nish Ghati, the Accounts Payable Clerk, to evaluate the costs of power supplies for the factory. There are six different options to be investigated and the Purchasing Manager would like Nish to carry out the analysis.

Identify the most appropriate response to this request. (Tick **one** option.)

(a)	The Purchasing Manager is in charge of purchasing decisions so the investigation should be carried out by the Purchasing team	
(b)	It is appropriate for the Accounts Payable Clerk to help if he has time available as the work should contribute to the solvency and cost effectiveness of the firm – these are key factors that the Accounts Department tries to control	
(c)	The Accounts Payable Clerk should help with this work, and the Finance Director should make the decision about the most appropriate power option, as he is responsible for the finances of the organisation	

(2 marks)

(d) In addition to running the monthly payroll, Leon Novak, the Payroll and General Ledger Clerk, is responsible for updating the non-current asset register and recording depreciation, as well as carrying out weekly bank reconciliations.

Identify whether each of the following statements is true or false.

Statements		**True**	**False**
(a)	There is an increased risk that non-current assets could be purchased for employee use		
(b)	A regular review of audit trails that show details of who originated each transaction will detect all frauds that have been carried out		
(c)	Simone Hyde, the Financial Accountant, should check the bank reconciliations to ensure that payroll amounts paid agree to authorised payroll prints		

(3 marks)

(e) Leon Novak, the Payroll and General Ledger Clerk, asks whether the following errors and omissions would be detected by carrying out a bank reconciliation. Identify whether each of these problems would or would not be detected by the reconciliation.

Problem		**Would be detected**	**Would not be detected**
(a)	Bank interest charged has been recorded in the cash book as bank interested received		
(b)	The bank has made a payment in error		
(c)	A customer has deducted a prompt payment discount to which they were not entitled		
(d)	A customer paid by BACS and did not email a remittance to EG Products Ltd		
(e)	A supplier was paid by both BACS and cheque		

(5 marks)

(f) A student from a local college was completing work experience with the Purchasing team. She took a phone call during which the caller claimed to be from a key supplier who had suffered a computer failure and had lost all its data. The caller asked for some key details of the supplier's contract with EGP, including quantities, prices, and discounts. The student provided the caller with the details as requested. The call turns out to have been bogus.

(i) Which of the fundamental ethical principles has been most clearly breached in this situation?

(Select from: Professional behaviour, Professional competence and due care, Confidentiality, Integrity, or Objectivity.)

(ii) Has the Data Protection Act been breached in this situation?

Yes / No

(2 marks)

Task 2: 20 marks

You have been asked to review the purchasing and payment procedures at EGP, and the adequacy of its controls over the general ledger.

(a) Identify whether each of the following activities would help ensure the information on the general ledger is accurate.

Activity		**Would help**	**Would not help**
(a)	Reports comparing actual revenues and costs against budget are produced each month		
(b)	Only authorised users can post journals in the general ledger		
(c)	The non-current asset register is reconciled to the general ledger periodically		
(d)	General ledger codes are reviewed and archived if not used for more than 24 months		
(e)	Inventory is counted periodically and compared to the inventory management system		

(5 marks)

Purchasing and payment procedures have remained unchanged for over five years – they were last updated when the current accounting system was installed. Although the systems are not formally documented, staff know and understand them well and problems or queries are usually resolved quickly.

Ordering raw materials and components

- Purchase requisitions are issued by the Stores Manager, for items constantly used by the Production department, or for items required for particular jobs.
- Purchase requisitions for items required for servicing or maintenance jobs are issued by the After-Sales Manager.
- The accounting system includes a purchase ordering module which is used by purchasing clerks to check purchase requisitions received against the computerised inventory records and against the quotes for future work on the job costing system. The purchasing clerks then create pre-numbered purchase orders using 'Approved Suppliers' and quoting the most recent agreed price for the component or material required.
- Purchase orders are printed, checked, and authorised by the Purchasing Manager, and then sent to suppliers in the post. A signed copy is sent to the accounts department for matching with invoices.

Receipts

- Deliveries of raw materials and components are dealt with by the stores department who check the quality of items received.
- Deliveries are matched to purchase orders, and stores staff update the inventory module of the accounting system for the goods received and create GRNs (Goods Received Notes).

Invoice approval and supplier account maintenance

- Nish Ghati, the Accounts Payable Clerk, is responsible for all updates to the payables ledger, both setting up suppliers and recording purchase invoices.
- Purchase invoices are matched to purchase orders and GRNs. Each invoice is stamped with a grid that requires details of the purchase order, the GRN number and the accounts code to which it is to be posted. These references must be entered, and all details matched for each reference before the accounting system allows the invoice to be posted.
- If invoices are sent by email, they are printed so that they can be stamped and checked.
- There is a folder of invoices awaiting processing because some, or all, details have not been matched to purchase orders and GRNs. This can lead to delays in paying invoices, and occasionally has resulted in EGP's account being put on stop with a supplier.
- Nish Ghati is responsible for investigating any discrepancies between purchase orders, deliveries, and invoices, arranging credit notes as appropriate, and for reconciling supplier statements received.
- Invoices are filed by month and then by supplier, and are archived after a couple of months.

Fuel and expenses

- Field engineers regularly need to travel to customer depots to carry out repairs or maintenance work onsite. The field engineers are given company credit cards to pay for fuel for their vehicles. These credit cards can also be used for one-off purchases of parts, and for accommodation should it be required.
- Engineers are required to keep receipts for all payments, and these are passed to Nish Ghati. He checks that all items on the credit card statements match with the receipts. He then codes the costs to the relevant jobs and files the statements with the other purchase invoices.

Payments

- An aged payables report is run by Nish Ghati twice a month to identify invoices due for payment.
- Simone Hyde, the Financial Accountant, checks the list and approves amounts to be paid. The list is passed to Amy Barton, the Assistant Accountant, who generates a BACS payment run, which is checked back to the approved list by Simone before she signs it off for payment. Because two signatures are required on BACS payments, one of the directors will also check and sign the list.
- Remittance advices are generated by Amy Barton and posted to suppliers.
- Urgent payments can be made by cheque, if required, but this is discouraged as it is a time consuming, more expensive, and a slower method of payment. Blank cheques are stored in Amy Barton's desk.

(b) **(i)** Identify FIVE systemic weaknesses in EGP's internal controls for purchasing and payments. (5 marks)

(ii) Explain how each weakness which you have identified could create a problem for the company. (10 marks)

Weakness	**Potential problem for the company**
1	
2	
3	
4	
5	

Task 3: 20 marks

EGP makes metal recycling containers, including one used for recycling for paper. Competition in the market for this product is increasing and Gloria Clarke, the Sales Director, feels that currently the containers are not competitively priced. In light of this, Martin Boyd, the Finance Director, has suggested that the business use target costing.

(a) Identify whether each of the following statements about target costing is true or false.

Statement	**True**	**False**
(a) Target costing includes all relevant costs of making a product		
(b) Target costing does not include overheads absorbed into production		
(c) Target costing is used to determine the price at which to sell the product		
(d) Target costing can be used as part of the value engineering process for a product		
(e) Target costing can only be used for new products		

(5 marks)

EGP is considering making a recycling container for Waste Electrical and Electronic Equipment (WEEE), to complement its existing product range.

Glenn MacArthur, the Production Director, has asked you to prepare some financial information on the new product.

The expected annual demand for the WEEE product is 500 units, although the popularity of these recycling containers may increase, according to the Sales Director.

EGP's estimated production costs for the WEEE recycling containers are as follows:

- Each container requires 380 kgs of steel, costing £1.30 per kg.
- It will take 11 hours of direct labour to produce each container at a cost of £18 per hour. New employees would be hired to build the new product.
- Existing supervisors would be expected to oversee production of the WEEE containers, and will receive additional production bonuses for this, totalling £6,000.
- Additional machinery would be required for production of the WEEE containers, costing £160,000. The depreciation on this machinery would be £32,000 per annum.
- Existing factory space currently costing £10,000 per annum could be used to produce the WEEE containers.

Glenn MacArthur's brother works for a business, Recycling Banks Limited, that produces WEEE recycling containers. Recycling Banks Limited can supply EGP with WEEE recycling containers at a price of £750 per container and has the capacity to produce up to 500 units per year. Recycling Banks Limited's products are generally good quality. However, its containers have been known to fail within the guarantee period and have had to be replaced, which has inconvenienced the customer. The administrative costs to EGP of dealing with any such failure are expected to total £1,500 per year.

(b) Calculate EGP's estimated production cost per unit for the WEEE recycling containers to the nearest £.

(5 marks)

Cost	**Amount £**

(c) From a purely financial perspective, evaluate whether EGP should produce WEEE recycling containers in-house or buy them from Recycling Banks Limited.

(6 marks)

(d) Identify four non-financial factors that EGP should consider before making a final decision on whether to make WEEE containers or buy them from Recycling Banks Limited.

(4 marks)

Task 4: 20 marks

One of EGP's suppliers, Casper Components Ltd, is in financial difficulties and needs an injection of capital. Casper Components Ltd contacts EGP to suggest that the company may like to consider investing in it.

Advantages to EGP would include being assured of preferential treatment as a customer of Casper Components Ltd, as well as being able to influence decisions made by the company – for instance, with regards to quality or product development. Casper Components Ltd requires an investment of £1 million.

(a) Use the extracts from the financial statements shown below to complete the calculation of financial ratios shown on the next page.

(10 marks)

Casper Components Ltd

Extracts from financial statements

Statement of profit or loss	**Year ended 30.6.20-5**	**Year ended 30.6.20-6**
	£000	£000
Revenue	18,861	20,748
Gross profit	6,601	7,054
Operating profit	1,225	990
Profit before tax	1,019	685
Statement of financial position		
Assets		
Non-current assets	3,918	4,214
Inventories	2,015	2,551
Trade receivables	2,429	2,785
Cash and cash equivalents	34	
Total assets	8,396	9,550
Equities and liabilities		
Equity	4,359	4,451
Non-current liabilities	2,575	3,350
Bank overdrafts		32
Trade payables	1,310	1,613
Taxation	152	104
Total equity and liabilities	8,396	9,550

Ratios

Complete the missing profitability, financial position, and liquidity ratios in the shaded cells of the table below, to one decimal place. Working capital ratios should be rounded to the nearest day.

Ratio	Year ended 30.6.20-5	Year ended 30.6.20-6
Profitability		
Gross profit margin %	35.0%	34.0%
Operating profit margin %	6.5%	4.8%
Return on capital employed %	17.7%	
Financial position		
Interest cover	5.9	2
Gearing	37.1%	
Liquidity		
Current ratio	3.1:1	3.1:1
Quick ratio/acid test	1.7:1	
Working capital management		
Inventory holding period	60 days	68 days
Trade receivables collection period	47 days	
Trade payables payment period	39 days	43 days
Working capital cycle	68 days	

(b) Select the **one** correct observation about each aspect of Casper Component Ltd's performance below.

(10 Marks)

Profitability

(a)	Casper Components Ltd profitability ratios have improved slightly	
(b)	The fall in the operating profit margin is caused by both the reduction in the gross profit margin and by the increase in operating expenses as a proportion of revenue	
(c)	Casper Components Ltd explains that it had to cut selling prices in 20-6 to boost sales, which accounts for the whole reduction in the firm's return on capital employed	

Financial position

(a)	The current level of interest cover is a significant cause for concern	
(b)	The current level of gearing indicates that the majority of the firm's finance is provided by loan finance	
(c)	Casper Components Ltd's increase in gearing indicates that the company has become riskier	

Liquidity

(a)	Casper Components Ltd's current and acid test ratios could indicate that working capital levels are too high	
(b)	The acid test/quick ratio has improved, indicating better management of working capital	
(c)	Although the acid test/quick ratio has declined, the current ratio has improved	

Working capital management

(a)	The working capital cycle has worsened. This change could be a consequence of overtrading	
(b)	The increased trade receivables collection period could have resulted from changes to credit terms or an increased focus on debt collection	
(c)	The increase in the trade payables payment period is a cause for concern	

Summary

(a)	EGP should not invest in Casper Components Ltd as the company cannot afford to service its current level of debt	
(b)	EGP's return on capital employed for the year ended 31 December 20-6 is 8.2%, so it should consider investing in Casper Components Ltd as it is currently generating a higher return than EGP	
(c)	EGP will be unable to access the funds required to invest in Casper Components Ltd, so cannot make this investment	

Task 5: 20 marks

Narissa Sealy, the Human Resources Director, is newly promoted to the role and is unclear why the Finance Department has so many staff. She has asked you to help her understand what the Finance function is responsible for, and also her responsibilities as a director.

(a) Identify whether each of the following statements in relation to the Finance function and the directors of a business is true or false.

Statement		**True**	**False**
(a)	The Finance function is the only part of the business responsible for the year-end financial statements		
(b)	The accounting systems should ensure EGP can comply with regulations, such as those imposed by HMRC		
(c)	The directors have a legal duty to stakeholders to behave ethically when producing financial reporting		
(d)	The directors are responsible for appointing auditors to audit the financial statements		
(e)	The directors are required by the Companies Act 2006 to produce financial statements under applicable accounting standards		

(5 marks)

Gloria Clarke, the Sales Director, is concerned that the maintenance and repairs part of the business is losing customers due to a lack of competitive pricing. The planning software used to schedule and raise sales invoices for repairs and maintenance is now several years old.

Gloria believes sales could be improved by implementing a new sales and planning system. An independent consultancy firm has investigated several systems at a cost of £4,700 and determined LogisticsPlus as the most appropriate system for EGP.

The LogisticsPlus system reviews and calculates the most appropriate route, adjusting it in real time where necessary, based on GPS information from tablets used by the field engineers. Field engineers will also use the tablets to record the parts used on the job, time spent, and also to raise the invoice. When repairs or maintenance is booked, customers are sent an email link that allows them to track when the work is due to take place.

Due to the complexity of the new system, new computer hardware and new tablets will need to be purchased at a cost of £15,400. The software licence for LogisticsPlus is £8,700 per year.

The field engineers will need IT training, as will two Finance staff. The initial training for the field engineers will take three days at a cost of £1,200 per day. The Finance staff will need to attend online training for half a day, costing £400 for each person. This will enable them to confirm that invoices transfer over correctly from LogisticsPlus into the accounting system.

The LogisticsPlus system is expected to reduce current transport costs of £68,000 per annum by 5%. It is expected to improve the field engineers' productivity by 3%. Field engineers currently cost £428,000 per annum. Gloria also expects customer sales to increase, as prices can be reduced because of these savings. However, she is not sure by how much sales would increase.

The LogisticsPlus system allows the field engineer to create a sales invoice at the end of the job, which is then authorised by the customer via the email link. An email detailing the parts that have been used is automatically sent to the Stores department, so that Stores can place a purchase order to replenish the parts used. The accounting system can be automatically updated by LogisticsPlus. This means that the Finance staff can reconcile the two systems, rather than creating the invoices individually as they do under the current system. This is expected to save the Accounts Receivable Clerk, Amy Barton, two days per month. Amy's salary, including employer costs, is £24,000 p.a.

(b) (i) Complete a financial cost-benefit analysis for the proposed LogisticsPlus forecasting and planning system, stating whether it is a net cost or benefit.

Costs	£
(Net cost) / benefit	

(6 marks)

(ii) Identify six non-financial factors that should be taken into account as part of the cost-benefit analysis.

(6 marks)

(iii) Recommend, with two reasons, whether the proposed investment should be made, or not.

(3 marks)

Answers to practice synoptic assessment 1

Task 1

(a) **(a)**, **(c)** and **(d)** are valid; **(b)** and **(e)** are not valid

(b) (b) Prepare the sales invoice as normal, but also keep a copy of the job sheet and send the original back to the relevant Branch Manager for investigation

(c) **(a)**, **(b)**, **(e)** and **(f)** would be detected; **(c)** and **(d)** would not be detected

(d) (e) All of the above

(e)

Policy	**Would promote**	**Would not promote**
Implement a price increase of 5% for all existing private customers when costs have increased by 2%		✓
Ask all qualified engineers to identify additional training requirements they have	✓	

(f) **Internal** information does not need to comply with accounting standards. If the business is planning to open more branches, **the directors** will make this type of decision. To monitor this decision, it will use **budgeted reports by branch**.

Task 2

(a) **(a)**, **(c)** and **(e)** would all help safeguard non-current assets and ensure they are accurately recorded.

(b) and **(d)** would not help safeguard non-current assets and ensure they are accurately recorded.

(b) Five of the following:

(i) Weaknesses	**(ii) Potential problem for the company**
Engineers' timesheets are filed at branch – no one at head office can check if hours are authorised or if hours input agree to the hours authorised.	Fraud risk – collusion between engineers and branch clerk could mean engineers could be paid for hours not worked. Errors could go unnoticed.
Payroll Clerk has full user rights.	Fraud risk - Payroll Clerk can change rates of pay, rates of pension contributions, or could add fictitious employees.
Branch managers can add temporary staff.	Fraud risk – fictitious employees could be added. Risk of breaching employment regulations if the branch manager does not carry out relevant checks, leading to fines.
Financial Accountant only has partial training on payroll software.	There may be inadequate cover if the Payroll Clerk is absent, which could mean staff may not get paid on time. Staff could have financial problems if they are paid late.
Financial Accountant checks are limited – no check of starters and leavers from payroll back to source documents, no check of deductions, or pension contributions.	Payroll Clerk's errors or fraud could go undetected.
No overall reconciliation from Userve to the payroll system for branch engineers' wages.	Payroll hours could be input incorrectly onto payroll system and engineers' wages overpaid or underpaid.
The Financial Accountant authorises the BACS payment.	Potential fraud by Financial Accountant as additional payments could be made and go undetected.

Other relevant points will attract marks.

Task 3

(a)

Statement	**True/False**
Value engineering is used to design new products and services at the lowest possible cost	False
Using value analysis on existing products will always result in the quality being kept the same or improved	True
Value engineering is used for both existing and new products	False
Value analysis considers how value is provided to the customer	True
Value engineering and value analysis focus on the elements of a product that do not contribute to the value of the product	True

(b)

Year	**0**	**1**	**2**	**3**	**4**
	£000	£000	£000	£000	£000
System development	-200	-150			
Marketing	-100	-50	-50	-50	-50
Sales revenue		5,600	4,200	2,100	700
Variable costs		-4,640	-3,480	-1,740	-580
Fixed costs		-80	-80	-80	-80
Net total for year	-300	680	590	230	-10
Discount factor 8%	1.000	0.926	0.857	0.794	0.735
Present value	-300	630	506	183	-7
Net present value					1,012

(c) Yes, ABL should undertake the development of the new system, as the net present value of its life cycle is positive: £1,012,000.

(d) This method of lifecycle costing requires all the costs and revenues to be estimated at the start of the project.

The research and design of the system are significant fixed costs, incurred at the start of the project, and will impact how the system is produced and, therefore, how much the variable costs will be. The life cycle cost indicates the research and design costs will be beneficial for ABL, but these initial costs will need to be planned for.

Demand for the new system is unknown, and estimates may be inaccurate and too high. It would be better to use a variety of demand assumptions to understand when sales would be so low that the development of the new system would be uneconomic.

Economies of scale may exist to reduce the variable cost per system over time. This would make the system more commercially appealing.

As this type of system becomes more well known, it may be possible to reduce the planned marketing spend, which is a fixed cost, thereby improving profitability.

The collection of costs and revenues by the accounting system over the lifecycle of the system is important to enable ABL to improve future budgeting for systems developments.

Task 4

(a)

Ratio	**Year ended 31.12.20-4**	**Year ended 31.12.20-5**
Return on capital employed	22.1%	**23.5%**
Gearing	11.9%	**10.9%**
Quick/acid test ratio	2.1:1	**2.2:1**
Inventory holding period	21 days	**21 days**
Working capital cycle	54 days	**54 days**

(b) **(i)** **Profitability**

This year, reductions in profit, caused by more sales at lower margin, have been successfully mitigated by careful management of overheads.

(ii) **Financial position**

Gearing has improved in 20-5, primarily due to the profits earned and retained in 20-5. The business is now less financially risky.

(iii) **Liquidity**

ABL has levels of liquidity that are very high. The money tied up in cash and trade receivables should be used elsewhere in the business.

(iv) **Working capital management**

The components of the working capital cycle are fairly constant. The trade receivables collection period has improved slightly and the trade payables payment period has deteriorated a little.

(v) **Overall performance**

The growth in the return on capital employed indicates an overall improvement in performance.

Task 5

(a)

Statement	**True/False**
Decision making will be faster, as the length of the scalar chain is shorter	False
The span of control is likely to be narrower	True
Productivity will be higher due to centralisation	True
A centralised structure is more expensive to operate	True
Branch managers will make more decisions under a centralised structure	False

(b) (i) Strengths

- Fuel purchasing system is robust, making fraud difficult and costs easy to monitor
- Capital expenditure is authorised by the directors and ordered using a unique purchase order number
- Purchase order system for capital expenditure matches deliveries and invoices to orders
- Experienced Purchasing Manager

(ii) Weaknesses

- No purchase order system linked to Userve
- No approved suppliers or standard cost information available on Userve
- Goods delivered to site may be of poor quality, but could still be paid for
- Lack of inventory controls over parts delivered to site
- Lack of accruals system in the financial statements for parts delivered not yet paid for
- Underpayment of plumbing and heating system suppliers by the Payables Ledger Clerk
- Delays in payment to suppliers
- Experienced Purchasing Manager due to retire next year
- Only one director approves capital expenditure purchases of over £1,000

(iii) Opportunities

- Centralised negotiation of prices, to reduce costs
- Use approved suppliers to increase discounts
- New purchase order add-on for Userve
- Recruit an employee to take over from the Purchasing Manager when he retires
- Train another staff member on quoting for microgeneration schemes

(iv) Threats

- Non-compliance with legislation for microgeneration schemes could lead to fines
- Overpayment of suppliers will mean financial statements are incorrect, and would adversely affect cash flow
- Inventory may be incorrectly valued, resulting in misstatement of profits and under or over payment of tax to HMRC

Any other relevant point for each of the four elements of the SWOT analysis may gain a mark.

(c) (i) & (ii)

Recommendation	Benefit
1 Purchase the purchase order add-on for Userve	**1** More accurate cost information **2** More efficient payment process for suppliers
2 Train another member of staff to be able to quote for microgeneration schemes	**1** Reduce burden of work and travelling on Steve **2** Increase sales of microgeneration schemes
3 Purchase goods centrally	**1** Improve discounts currently available **2** Improve controls over purchasing
4 Implement a more robust capital expenditure authorisation procedure - for example, spend of £5,000 or more requires approval from two directors	**1** Capital expenditure will be considered in light of all business needs, not just those of one director **2** Cash flow will improve as large purchases will be planned for

(d) ABL has fitted microgeneration systems that it knows were non-compliant and has not informed its regulatory body.

Answers to practice synoptic assessment 2

Task 1

(a) (a) Companies Act 2006

(d) Accounting standards

(b) (d) Strong organisational controls

(c) (d) The Human Resources Director

(d)

Error or discrepancy		**Would be detected**	**Would not be detected**
(a)	Miscoding of a petty cash voucher as travel rather than subsistence		✔
(b)	Theft of cash from the petty cash tin	✔	
(c)	Petty cash claims have been paid for more than the maximum amount allowed		✔
(d)	Addition error on petty cash voucher		✔
(e)	Clerical error resulting in the wrong amount of petty cash being paid out	✔	

(e) Human error: (e) Sense checks which prevent the posting of transactions dated outside the current period

Power failure: (c) Automatic back-ups

(f) Professional competence and due care

(g) (c) Ensure any work performed is supervised and reviewed by the Payroll Clerk

Task 2

(a)

Internal control	**Purpose**	**Suitable Yes / No**
Regularly reconcile the VAT control account	Prevent and detect fraud and error	Yes
The directors are the only authorised signatories on the bank accounts	Compliance	No
The new accounting system is cloud based and is backed up automatically	Facilitate operations	Yes

(b)

Internal control	**Cash-based**	**Credit-based**
Customers are subject to rigorous credit checks with a credit agency prior to orders being placed		✔
Customers pay for the goods at the point of order and collection	✔	

(c) Any five of the following:

(i) Weakness	**(ii) Potential problems for the company**
Sales staff should check the status of an account before accepting an order – but if they are busy, or only interested in achieving their sales targets, they may not do this. It is possible for an order to be placed even if an account is over its credit limit, overdue, or on stop.	Sale to a bad credit risk, and subsequent irrecoverable debt.
Human error is possible when the sales order worksheets are completed – this could lead to orders being under- or over-priced. VAT might not be charged when applicable, or could be charged on orders for which a zero rate applies.	Errors in pricing or amounts of VAT could cause disputes with customers. If a lower price is quoted than should have been, the company will probably have to honour this price which may result in the sale being loss-making.
Human error could lead to delays in some sales orders being emailed to production, or for some sales to be missed completely so production is not informed.	Customers will be dissatisfied if goods are received late, or not received at all. This could cause them to change to other suppliers. Production will find it difficult to schedule output effectively if orders are not notified promptly.
No despatch notes produced for customers to sign - customers could deny having received the goods.	CDM will not be able to prove goods have been delivered, and will then struggle to make the customer pay.
Details of some despatches might not be emailed to the Receivables Ledger Clerk, or there may be a delay in emailing details of goods despatched.	Sales might not be invoiced, causing loss to the company. Sales might be invoiced late – this will affect cash flow as payments will be made based on invoice date, rather than delivery date.
The Receivables Ledger Clerk is responsible for creating all invoices and credit notes.	If the clerk colluded with a customer, invoices could never be raised. Alternatively, the clerk could issue credit notes against amounts outstanding in return for payments from customers.

Other relevant points may also gain marks.

Task 3

(a)

Statement	**True / False**
Revenues are likely to be highest in the growth stage of the product	False
The learning effect is likely to reduce costs in the growth and maturity stages	True
The majority of costs will be fixed in the development stage	True
Higher automation costs should only be incurred if production costs fall as a result	True
Marketing costs will continue to be high in the maturity stage	False

(b) **(i)**

	Grade A Barley	**Grade B barley**
Variable cost per tonne, £	205	185
Contribution per tonne, £	45	40

(ii) Grade A barley first, grade B barley second

(iii) All finished goods inventory could be sent out to customers to fulfil the orders, rather than holding some as inventory.

As CDM has two plants, it could move production of Grade B barley to the Lincolnshire plant.

The business could try to identify supplies of similar quality Grade A or Grade B barley and purchase from them to fulfil the orders.

CDM could contact customers to see if they can accept delayed, or phased, deliveries.

Staff could be asked to work overtime to make extra processing time available to meet the orders for both grades of barley.

Other relevant points may also gain marks.

(iv) If orders for Grade B barley cannot be met, customers may move their business elsewhere.

If all finished goods inventory is all used this month, the business may be unable to fulfil future peaks in demand, or deal with a loss of machine processing time in future months.

The additional transportation and distribution costs associated with moving production to Lincolnshire may significantly reduce the contribution per tonne for both products.

Increased overtime costs will reduce the contribution per tonne for Grade B barley further.

Other relevant points should gain marks.

Task 4

(a)

Ratio	Year ended 30.12.20-5	Year ended 30.12.20-6
Operating profit margin %	7.8%	**9.1%**
Interest cover	2.3 times	**1.8 times**
Gearing	35.6%	**60.0%**
Current ratio	1.4:1	**1.6:1**
Trade payables payment period	122 days	**111 days**
Working capital cycle*	41 days	**53 days**

*Working capital cycle has not been asked for but needs to be calculated to answer the question on working capital management.

(b) Profitability

(c) The improvement in the gross profit margin and the operating profit margin could not have been achieved if costs had increased in line with revenue

Financial position

(c) The business has gone from having medium levels of gearing in 20-5 to high levels of gearing in 20-6

Liquidity

(a) Both liquidity ratios have improved over the year

Working capital management

(c) The change in the trade payables payment period indicates a lack of financial control

Overall performance

(b) Although underlying profitability has improved in 20-6, the level of gearing and resultant interest costs are a significant cause for concern

Task 5

(a)

Statement	True	False
Only relevant costs should be included in the make or buy decision	✔	
The quality of the bought-in product will always be as good as what CDM can produce		✔
The reliability of supply should be considered as part of the decision-making process	✔	
Production overheads currently absorbed into CDM's partly-processed products should be included in the cost comparison of making or buying the product		✔
The only consideration in the decision should be financial		✔

(b) **(i)**

Costs	£
Training costs (£1,600 x 4 staff) + (£800 x 2 staff)	8,000
Loading existing contracts onto the new system	6,000
Software licence	15,000
Hardware upgrades	17,500
Benefits	
Cost saving of grain purchases (£12,400,000 x 0.5%)	62,000
Overtime saved	3,000
(Net cost)/benefit	18,500 benefit

(ii) Any six from:

- Will the buyers be unhappy to lose the overtime which they have been paid for several years?
- Will the buyers and directors be able to use the new system effectively?
- Will the forecasting be more accurate and the anticipated savings in grain purchases be achieved?
- Will the IT training be sufficient to meet the needs of the staff?
- How will the transition to the new forecasting system be managed?
- What controls will be in place to load in the existing contracts?
- Information reported by the new system is more extensive, so should enable better decision-making.

(iii) Any two from:

CDM should invest in the GrainStore system, as:

- It should result in a net benefit of £18,500.
- It should reduce grain purchase costs.
- It should improve decision-making on purchases, due to better reporting information.

Answers to practice synoptic assessment 3

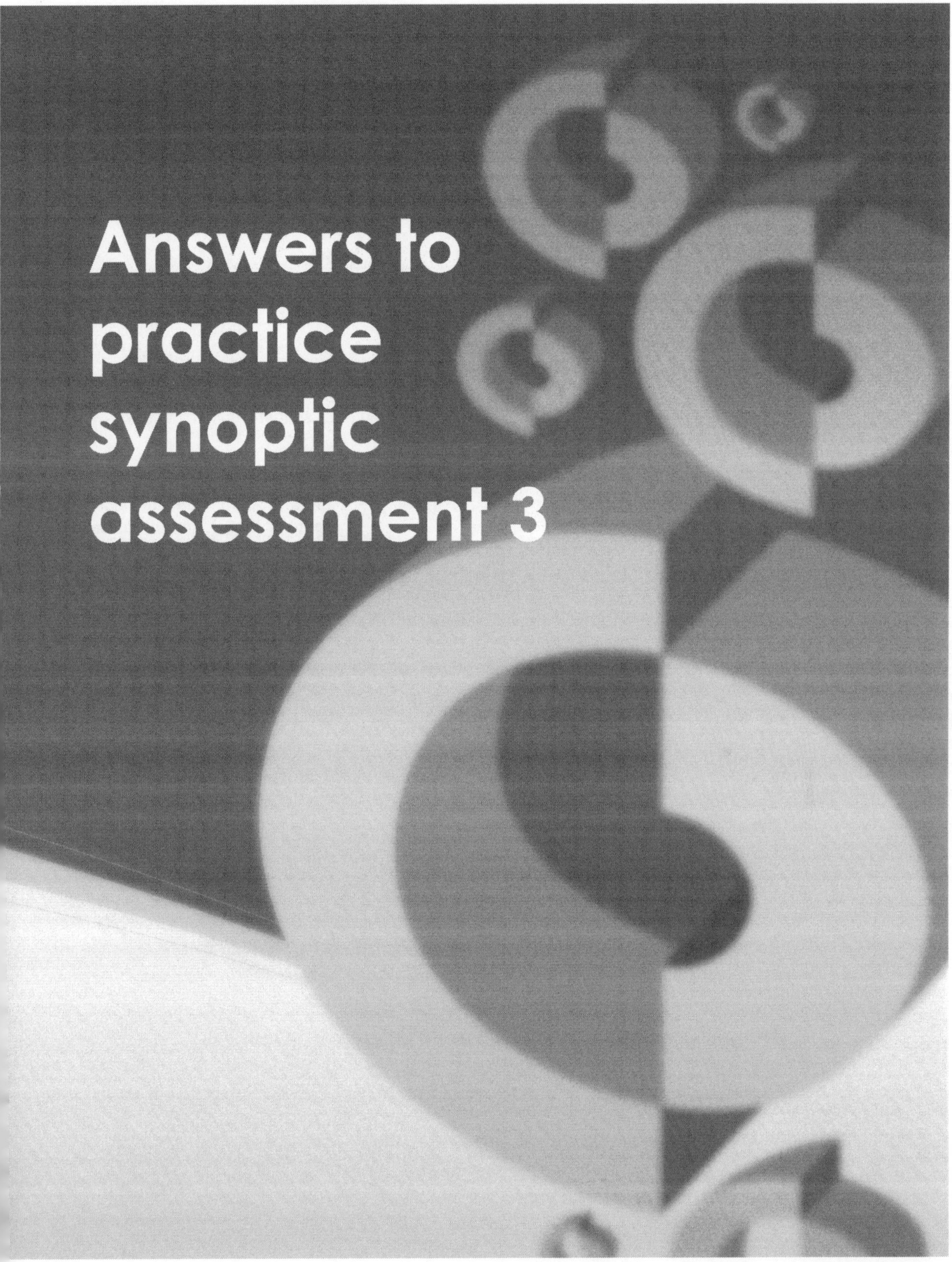

Task 1

(a)

	Lenders	Credit customers	Shareholders
To assess potential for future growth		✔	
To assess security for borrowings	✔		
To assess potential for future dividend payments			✔

(b) (c) Advise Kris Lewinski, the Assistant Accountant, of the error so that it can be rectified

(c)

Situation		Would result in the error that has been detected	Would not result in the error that has been detected
(a)	Receipt of goods incorrectly recorded as 100 units instead of 1,000 units		✔
(b)	Theft of items from stores	✔	
(c)	An issue from stores to production incorrectly recorded as 100 units instead of 1,000 units	✔	
(d)	A container of goods on the production line was counted twice		✔
(e)	Inventory records not updated for disposal of out-of-date inventory	✔	

(d) (b) Accounting system will not accept transactions with a date in the future

(d) Users only have access to the parts of the system required for their job

(e) Credit notes need to be raised by one of the clerks and checked by Hannah Cobb, the Financial Accountant, before they are approved for posting

(g) Journals are entered by qualified accounts personnel

(e) Integrity

(f) Close the cash book as normal

(g) True

Task 2

(a)

Description		**Internal control**
(a)	Ensuring employees have appropriate qualifications for their job	Personnel
(b)	Credit notes are raised by the Accounts Payable Clerk and signed off by the Financial Accountant	Authorisation
(c)	Variances between actual and budget are investigated each month	Management
(d)	Supplier statements are regularly reconciled with the payables ledger	Arithmetic & accounting
(e)	Vehicle registration documents are kept in a locked cabinet in the Finance Director's office	Physical

(b) Five of the following:

Weakness	**Potential problem for the company**
Customers are not credit checked before credit is given	Sale to a bad credit risk and subsequent irrecoverable debt
No formal credit agreements are produced for signature by the customer before trading commences	Lack of clarity over terms of trade. Possible problems may arise should disputes with customers need to be resolved with legal action
There are no agreed credit limits	No limit on potential irrecoverable debt risk
Staff do not check the current balance or status of a customer's account before accepting an order	Sale may be made to a customer who is a bad credit risk, which may result in a subsequent irrecoverable debt
No defined debt collection policy	Staff will take an ad hoc approach if issues arise. Staff have no guidance about what action should be taken if a credit customer fails to pay, and when it should be taken.
No member of staff is responsible for monitoring customer accounts and chasing debts, ie credit control	Problems may not be detected for a long time. Customers who delay payment will not be chased. This may encourage late payment by customers who could afford to pay but want to improve their own cash flow
No procedures for putting customers' accounts on stop	Sales may continue to be made to customers with liquidity issues who cannot pay. This will affect the liquidity of FBL and, should these debts ultimately be irrecoverable, also its profitability
Invoices and statements are posted to customers	This is expensive and slow compared with emailing these documents. It is also not environmentally friendly

Any other relevant points may attract marks.

Task 3

(a)

Statement		**True**	**False**
(a)	The unit cost comparison of make or buy should only include additional costs incurred when making the product	✔	
(b)	The only factor to consider in the make or buy decision is the unit cost per product		✔
(c)	Significant variations in volume could have an impact on whether to make or buy the products	✔	
(d)	Fixed factory overheads absorbed by the products currently being made will need to be absorbed elsewhere if a business buys or outsources	✔	
(e)	The quality of the products will always be the same, if made or outsourced		✔

(b) **(i)** £180,000 ÷ 90 = **£2,000** per recipe.

(ii) £2,000 ÷ 24 days ÷ 1,000 litres x 100p = **8.33** pence per litre of soup.

(iii) £2,000 ÷ 300 days ÷ 7,000 x 100p = **0.10** pence per sausage roll.

(iv) A significant part of the cost of a manufactured product is made up of the overheads allocated to it. Therefore, it is important to get an accurate picture of how much overhead each product is responsible for.

Activity-based costing will give FBL more accurate overhead costs for each product, and so more accurate total product costs.

Decisions about the selling prices and profitability of different products will be based on more accurate information.

Loss-making products will be more clearly identified, and decisions can be made whether to discontinue them or to increase their selling prices.

FBL is in a price competitive industry, so more accurate costing and pricing may lead to FBL being more competitively priced, resulting in higher sales for some products.

(c) Activity-based costing requires more data collection than absorption costing, so will be more time-consuming to implement and maintain.

Staff will require significant training, possibly on specialist software, to be able to carry out activity-based costing, which they may find difficult to understand and use correctly.

FBL may not benefit significantly by implementing activity-based costing, as a large proportion of its operating costs are likely to be direct, rather than indirect, due to the nature of its products.

The number of products FBL has is growing, so an activity-based system will require significant resources to ensure that it remains accurate and up-to-date.

Task 4

(a)

Ratio	**Company overall**	**High street shop**	**New out of town shop**
Profitability			
Gross profit margin %	38.00%	**34.96%**	39.13%
Operating profit margin %	2.91%	1.03%	**5.22%**
Asset turnover (net assets)	4.63 times	**7.48 times**	2.21 times
Return on capital employed	13.47%	7.69%	**11.54%***
Inventory holding period	16 days	**12 days**	8** days

*the new store has only been open for 6 months; full year's operating profit = 2 x 12 = 24, so ROCE = 24÷208 x100 = 11.54%

**the new shop has only been open for 6 months; full year's cost of sales = 6 ÷ (230 - 90 x 2), so inventory holding period = 6 ÷ 280 x 365 = 8 days

(b)

(i) The gross profit margin is worse for the high street shop than the new out of town shop

(ii) If more out of town shops were opened, the company's overall operating profit margin would increase, based on this information

(iii) The asset turnover (net assets) for the new out of town shop may be depressed because of the value of recently purchased land and buildings

(iv) The return on capital employed for the company is better than the high street shop's return on capital employed

(v) The inventory holding periods for both shops are lower for than the company overall, as inventory is held at the factory

(c)

Key performance indicator	**Factor causing the KPI to get worse**
Gross profit margin %	Reduced selling prices
Operating profit margin %	Increased overheads
Asset turnover (net assets)	Reduced revenue
Return on capital employed	Increased capital employed
Inventory holding period	Purchase of raw materials due to discounts offered

Task 5

(a)

Internal control	Small	Medium	Large
Exception reporting is used to investigate tills where discrepancies between cash takings and till information are higher than £5 per till, per shift			✔
Shop managers are responsible for compliance with food hygiene certification by staff employed in the shop	✔*		
When the Regional Sales Manager visits a shop, they review the value of wastage for the last month		✔**	
Shop managers will set product promotions, and monitor their success	✔		
At a specific time of day, certain products are reduced in price, via the till software			✔

*medium and large organisations are likely to control this risk centrally

**this would not be needed in a small organisation. A large organisation would monitor this by shop on a daily basis

(b) Any two for each of the four categories:

Strengths

- Accounting software package used is efficient
- Accounting software ensures compliance with RTI requirements
- Changes to tax rates and allowances are adjusted through automatic updates
- Good segregation of duties between HR who set up and remove employees on the payroll system, and the Payroll Clerk who records the hours worked
- Payment of wages by BACS is secure and cost effective
- Bank charges for automated payments are lower than for cash or cheque payments

Weaknesses

- Reliance on shop managers to identify optimum staffing level for their shops
- Reliance on shop managers to transfer clocking data to a USB and then email it to the Payroll Clerk
- Smart cards can be given to co-workers who could fraudulently clock in for an employee who is not at work. The employee would be paid for hours not worked.
- Shop managers are responsible for notifying HR of leavers and may delay doing this, so ex-employees continue to be paid fraudulently

Opportunities

- FBL could invest in a workforce management system to better manage its staff cost
- FBL could upgrade its clocking system to use biometric data for employees to log in and out by using their fingerprint
- FBL could integrate the clocking system with the accounting software system so that data is transferred directly to the Payroll Clerk

Threats

- FBL could be at risk of legal proceedings if shop managers fail to apply employment law properly
- Financial accounts could be incorrect
- Overpayment of staff for hours not worked

Any other valid point would also earn marks.

(c) **(i) & (ii)**

Recommendations	**Benefits**
Regional sales managers could analyse staffing levels at different stores.	Shop staffing levels would be optimised. Shops would work more efficiently, and profitability would increase.
The clocking in system could be upgraded and integrated with the payroll system.	Time would be saved by shop managers. The risk of data loss and incorrect information being included in the accounts would be reduced.
Replace the current clocking in/out system with one that uses biometric measures.	Only staff who are working would be able to clock in and get paid, reducing the risk of fraud and increasing profitability. Health and safety records of who is on site would be accurate.
Regional managers could carry out unannounced visits and check staff who are working.	Fictitious shop workers would be identified. Shop managers would be deterred from committing this type of fraud.

Any other valid recommendation and benefit would also earn marks.

(d) Any one of:

- Internal training courses
- External training courses
- Online courses
- Telephone support lines

Answers to practice synoptic assessment 4

Task 1

(a) **(a)** and **(c)** Purchasing team; **(b)** and **(d)** Accounts Department

(b) **(a)** and **(b)** do not include in the cash flow, **(c)** and **(d)** include in the cash flow

(c) (b)

(d) **(a)** and **(b)** are false; **(c)** is true

(e) **(a)**, **(b)** and **(d)** would be detected; **(c)** and **(e)** would not

(f) **(i)** Confidentiality

(ii) Yes

Task 2

(a) **(a)**, **(b)** and **(c)** would help; **(d)** and **(e)** would not

(b)

Weakness	**Potential problem for the company**
Purchasing systems and procedures are not documented.	New staff, or those working to cover staff who are absent or unwell, are less likely to be able to operate efficiently and could make mistakes, such as approving invoices which are charging too much for goods, or for which no goods have been received.
The Accounts Payable Clerk is responsible for creating supplier accounts, recording invoices and reconciling supplier statements. There is no segregation of duties.	The Accounts Payable Clerk could commit fraud by creating bogus suppliers, recording fictitious invoices from them, and then paying himself. The Accounts Payable Clerk could also commit fraud by colluding with a genuine supplier to record invoices for which goods have never been received. The Accounts Clerk could also make mistakes, overpaying suppliers, which no one would find.
The Accounts Payable Clerk is responsible for entering all supplier details when setting up, or amending, supplier details.	Potential for fraud, as the Accounts Payable Clerk could change supplier bank details to a bank account which he controls.
Credit card statements are only checked back to receipts; the validity of receipts is not checked.	Potential for fraud, as field engineers could use credit cards to pay for fuel for their personal use or for personal expenses. As their costs are charged to the jobs they work on, this will make EGP's charges to customers more expensive and could lead to it losing contracts.

There is no check of fuel usage or mileage against the location of jobs.	Potential for fraud, as field engineers could be using credit cards to pay for fuel for their own vehicles.
There are delays in recording purchase invoices received when all details do not match exactly with purchase orders and goods received records.	Payments to suppliers could be late which could lose supplier goodwill and reduce potential prompt payment discounts. Monthly management accounts may not be accurate as these invoices are not automatically accrued for.
Remittance advices are posted to suppliers.	This is slow, more expensive (postage and stationery costs) and not good for the environment, as it uses paper and requires delivery vehicles.
Blank cheques are stored in a desk.	The cheques could be stolen and used to commit fraud against the company.

Task 3

(a) **(a)** and **(d)** are true, **(b)**, **(c)** and **(e)** are false

(b)

Cost	**Amount £**
Direct materials: 380 kgs x £1.30 per kg	494
Direct labour:11 hrs x £18/hr	198
Supervisor costs: £6,000 / 500 units	12
Machinery depreciation: £32,000 / 500 units	64
Total	**768**

Note: the factory space is not relevant to this calculation.

(c)

Cost if purchased from Recycling Banks Limited	Amount £
Unit cost	750
Administrative costs: £1,500 / 500 units	3
Total	**753**

Based on sales of 500 WEEE recycling containers per year, it would be cheaper to purchase them from Recycling Banks Limited, rather than build them in-house.

However, the estimated sales volume is uncertain, and should the actual volume be higher than estimated, the depreciation on the machinery would be spread over additional units, making the cost per unit lower. For example, if 1,000 units were produced using the same machinery, the depreciation cost would reduce to £32 per unit. If supervisor costs could be kept at £12 per unit, the revised cost per unit would be £736; £17 cheaper than the cost of buying in from Recycling Banks Limited.

Alternatively, the sales volume may turn out to be lower than 500 units, so the supervisor bonuses may be avoided. However, the depreciation cost per unit would then increase, meaning it is likely that EGP's cost of production would then significantly exceed that of the buy in cost from Recycling Banks Limited.

As Recycling Banks Limited is only able to supply a maximum of 500 WEEE recycling containers, EGP's profits for this product will be limited by this should sales exceed that level.

(d) The difference between the costs of EGP and Recycling Banks Limited is small, so other factors may be more significant in the 'make or buy' decision.

The cost per kg of steel used to make the containers could be unpredictable. If EGP purchased the containers from Recycling Banks Limited at a pre-agreed set price, the risk of any changes in steel costs would be with Recycling Bank Limited, not EGP.

Production in-house by EGP relies on it being able to recruit new staff to make the product. This may take more time, cost more, and require more training than anticipated, all of which could have a negative impact on profitability. The period of employment for the new staff would also need to be considered – would these be permanent posts or fixed term contracts?

The cost of purchasing additional machinery will also be significant. EGP should consider the impact on cash flow of this purchase and whether the machinery could be redeployed elsewhere in the business, should the WEEE recycling containers prove unpopular.

Recycling Banks Limited has previously had quality issues with its products. To limit the possible impact of this, EGP would need to carry out rigorous quality checks prior to sending this product to customers. If EGP feels its reputation could be damaged by any failures of Recycled Banks Limited's products, it should make the product in-house, or find another, more reliable, supplier.

Glenn MacArthur, the Production Director, appears to have a conflict of interest, as his brother works for Recycling Banks Limited. This should be resolved prior to any contracts being agreed.

Task 4

(a)

Ratio	**Year ended 30.6.20-5**	**Year ended 30.6.20-6**
Return on capital employed %	17.7%	**12.7%**
Gearing	37.1%	**42.9%**
Quick ratio/acid test	1.7:1	**1.6:1**
Trade receivables collection period	47 days	**49 days**
Working capital cycle	68 days	**74 days**

(b) **Profitability**

(b) The fall in the operating profit margin is caused by both the reduction in the gross profit margin and by the increase in operating expenses as a proportion of revenue

Financial position

(c) Casper Components Ltd's increase in gearing indicates that the company has become riskier

Liquidity

(a) Casper Components Ltd's current ratios and acid test ratios could indicate working capital levels are too high

Working capital management

(a) The working capital cycle has worsened. This change could be a consequence of overtrading

Summary

(b) EGP's return on capital employed for the year ended 31 December 20-6 is 8.2%, so it should consider investing in Casper Components Ltd as it is currently generating a higher return than EGP

Task 5

(a) **(a)**, **(c)**, and **(d)** are false, **(b)** and **(e)** are true

(b) **(i)**

Costs	£
Computer hardware and tablets	15,400
Software licence	8,700
Field engineer training (3 days x £1,200 per day)	3,600
Finance staff training (2 staff x £400)	800
Benefits	
Reduction in transport costs (£68,000 x 5%)	3,400
Productivity saving (£428,000 x 3%)	12,840
Time saved by Finance (£24,000 x 24/365)	1,578
(Net cost) / benefit	(10,682) Cost

(ii) Six from:

- The new system will remove current inefficiencies, such as individual invoicing by Finance.
- Customers will benefit from better customer service, via real time information, as they can track the field engineers.
- Productivity savings may, or may not, result in cost savings, depending on whether field engineers are used on new jobs, or simply underutilised.
- Sales may increase if prices can be reduced due to cost savings.
- Field engineers may find it difficult to use the new LogisticsPlus system, which could result in invoices not being raised correctly, or at all.
- Staff morale and motivation may reduce while the new system is implemented.
- The implementation period may lead to temporary inefficiencies.
- The customer authorises the repair, providing proof of delivery.
- Stores are informed of the parts used, but LogisticsPlus does not integrate with the parts ordering system.

Marks will be given for other appropriate answers.

(iii) Even though the net cost of the system is £10,682, EGP should invest in the LogisticsPlus system, as this is a relatively small investment.

The improvements in customer service and automated invoicing will make the business more efficient and will differentiate it from its competitors. This may then have a positive impact on sales.

Marks will be given for other appropriate answers.